STITCHED FROM THE HEART

QUILTS AND MORE TO GIVE WITH LOVE

Kori Turner-Goodhart

Martingale®
Create with Confidence

Stitched from the Heart: Quilts and More to Give with Love
© 2019 by Kori Turner-Goodhart

Martingale®
19021 120th Ave. NE, Ste. 102
Bothell, WA 98011-9511 USA
ShopMartingale.com

Printed in China
24 23 22 21 20 19   8 7 6 5 4 3 2 1

Library of Congress Cataloging-in-Publication Data is available upon request.

ISBN: 978-1-60468-992-1

MISSION STATEMENT

We empower makers who use fabric and yarn
to make life more enjoyable.

CREDITS

**PUBLISHER AND
CHIEF VISIONARY OFFICER**
Jennifer Erbe Keltner

CONTENT DIRECTOR
Karen Costello Soltys

DESIGN MANAGER
Adrienne Smitke

MANAGING EDITOR
Tina Cook

PRODUCTION MANAGER
Regina Girard

TECHNICAL EDITOR
Amelia Johanson

PHOTOGRAPHER
Brent Kane

COPY EDITOR
Sheila Chapman Ryan

ILLUSTRATOR
Christine Erikson

SPECIAL THANKS
*Photography for this book was taken at the
home of Kirsten Yanasak of Everett, Washington.
Instagram: @brightyellowdoor*

DEDICATION

*My mom told me, "If you work hard enough,
Kori, you can make all your dreams come true."
This book is for my daughter, Jaye Anne.
This is what it looks like when dreams come true, little love.*

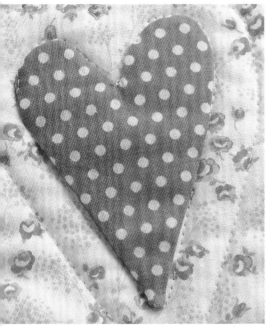

CONTENTS

Introduction

Giving gifts is one of my favorite acts of kindness. A gift can empower, comfort, show love, inspire, and teach. Something you make and give can be cherished as an heirloom for generations to come. But the most brilliant thing about a gift is that it offers as much to the giver as to the receiver. Few things are as priceless as seeing joy on a friend or loved one's face, followed by that look that seems to be saying, *"How does she know me so well?"*

In this book you'll find nine heartfelt projects for all sorts of different occasions. These are special sewn items you can give to brides, graduates, babies, or even someone who just needs a pick-me-up. Each gift is designed to be stitched with love.

When I started dreaming up these projects, I wanted to be sure they could be tailored for *your* loved ones by combining hand embroidery, hand appliqué, and simple patchwork. The backgrounds are simple, but the embroidery stitches and personalization you can add make these charming projects come to life. I've included my handwritten alphabet in a couple of sizes that you can use to personalize each piece, but I encourage you to be courageous and use your own handwriting to make your gifts even more special. There's just something sincere about including your own handwriting. Also, feel free to make the projects in your own favorite fabrics. While my happy vintage style shows in every design, make a project uniquely yours by working with bold batiks or Civil War reproduction prints—whatever style you love.

From the bottom of my heart, I hope this book inspires you to spread joy, happiness, smiles, and, most importantly, love. Giving a handmade gift to someone is opening your soul. And while my intent is to provide a selection of beautiful gifts to make for others, I'll be just as delighted if you make one or two for yourself—consider it my gift to you.

Fondly,

Kori

BELOVED BED RUNNER

Designed and made by Kori Turner-Goodhart. Quilted by Linda Sekerak.

 Two darling little appliquéd birds and some sweet hand embroidery make this bed runner the ideal wedding or anniversary gift. A simple patchwork background lets you pick a selection of dreamy fabrics to complement the featured handwork.

FINISHED BED RUNNER: 18½" × 60½"

MATERIALS

Yardage is based on 42"-wide fabric. Fat eighths measure 9" × 21".

⅞ yard of polka-dot linen for background

5 fat eighths of assorted gray prints for border

⅛ yard of green mottled print for grass*

⅞ yard of red diagonal stripe for bird bodies and binding

1 rectangle, at least 9" × 20", of red print for bird wings and tail feathers

1 rectangle, at least 9" × 12", of taupe floral for bird faces and bellies

2 rectangles, at least 9" × 20" *each,* of different cream prints for tulips

2 rectangles, at least 9" × 20" *each,* of different green prints for tulip leaves

4 rectangles, at least 9" × 12" *each,* of assorted light blue fabrics for clouds

1" × 30" strip of green solid for tulip stems

*I used a green Grunge print by Basic Grey for Moda Fabrics.

Small scrap of orange check for bird beaks

1⅞ yards of fabric for backing

25" × 67" piece of batting

Cosmo Seasons variegated floss in brown #5030; taupe #5028; rust orange #5007; purple #8066; green #5014; and mint green #5016

Cosmo solid floss in red #346 and charcoal #895

Eleganza pearl cotton #8 in Up a Tree #EZM09

Black Pigma Micron pen .01 (fine tip)

Glue stick (optional)

WHAT'S GRUNGE GOT TO DO WITH IT?

Grunge fabrics are dyed first, and then printed on one side for muted effect. They're part of Moda Fabrics' Basic Grey line, and they're perfect for achieving the vintage flavor captured in my patterns.

CUTTING

From the polka-dot linen, cut:
3 rectangles, 12½" × 20½"

From *each* of the 5 assorted gray prints, cut:
8 squares, 3½" × 3½" (40 total)

From the binding fabric, cut:
5 strips, 2½" × 42"

FLOSS GUIDE

Use two strands of floss for all stitching unless otherwise noted.

- ✖ **Brown:** Snail body, sky birds
- ✖ **Charcoal:** Bird eyes (three wraps) and brows
- ✖ **Green:** Leaf details
- ✖ **Mint green:** Cloud accents
- ✖ **Purple:** Snail shell, tulip head details, tulip head heart
- ✖ **Taupe:** Bird wings, tail feathers and accents (three wraps), tail swirl
- ✖ **Red:** Bird outline
- ✖ **Rust orange:** Bird feet and details (three wraps)
- ✖ **Up a Tree:** Fern stem, fern leaves and veins, grass outline

PIECING THE APPLIQUÉ BACKGROUND

Join the three polka-dot linen 12½" × 20½" rectangles in a horizontal row as shown, using a ¼" seam allowance, to make a bed-runner background panel that measures 12½" × 60½", including seam allowances. Press the seam allowances open.

Make 1 panel, 12½" × 60½".

ADDING THE APPLIQUÉ AND EMBROIDERY

The appliqué and embroidery patterns are on pages 10–12. Refer to "Stitch-and-Flip Appliqué" on page 75 for detailed information, or prepare your appliqué shapes for your favorite method. Embroidery stitches are diagrammed on pages 73 and 74.

1. Cut and prepare the bird, tulip, leaf, and cloud appliqués.

2. Prepare the grass by cutting off the selvages of the green mottled print. Fold the strip in half lengthwise, right sides together. Draw a grass line by hand onto the fabric. Since grass is organic, you can make your line as rolling or straight as you like. Stitch on the line, and then finish preparing the grass referring to the stitch-and-flip technique.

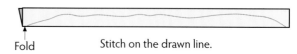

Fold   Stitch on the drawn line.

3. Use the green solid 1" × 30" strip to make a ¼"-wide strip. Crosscut the strip to make six stems, ¼" × 4½", as shown.

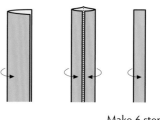

Make 6 stems,
¼" × 4½".

4. Lay out the prepared appliqués on the background panel according to the appliqué placement guide. Note that the clouds extend off both sides of the runner; they will be trimmed later. For the four inner tulips, slip the lower edge of the stems under the grass. For the two outer tulips, align the tulip leaves and stems with the lower edge of the background panel so the leaves and stems will be caught in the seam of the lower border when it's attached. Pin or use a glue stick to secure all of the appliqués for stitching.

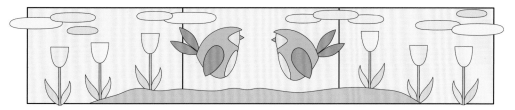

Appliqué placement

5. Hand appliqué all the pieces to the background panel and press flat.

6. Using the Pigma pen, trace the embroidery details (with the aid of a light box) onto the appliqué shapes and background panels. Hand embroider the details to complete the bed-runner center. For specific floss colors, refer to the "Floss Guide" on page 8. Finish the grass edge with a blanket stitch and pearl cotton.

7. Once the embroidery is complete, press the bed-runner center flat. Trim the cloud appliqués even with the sides of the runner.

ASSEMBLING THE BED RUNNER

Press the seam allowances as indicated by the arrows.

1. Lay out 20 assorted gray 3½" squares in a row. Stitch the squares together to make a row that measures 3½" × 60½", including seam allowances. Repeat for a second row.

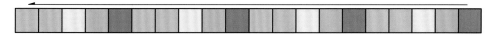

Make 2 rows, 3½" × 60½".

2. Join the pieced rows to the top and bottom of the bed-runner center as shown. The bed runner should measure 18½" × 60½".

Bed-runner assembly

FINISHING THE BED RUNNER

For more details on any finishing steps, visit ShopMartingale.com/HowtoQuilt for free, downloadable information.

1. Layer the runner top, batting, and backing. Hand or machine quilt as desired. The bed runner shown is machine quilted in whimsical swirls and a feather pattern. The pieced borders feature a flower motif in each square. Trim the excess batting and backing even with the quilt top.

2. Join the red stripe 2½"-wide binding strips end to end to make one long strip. Use this strip to make double-fold binding and attach it to the runner.

Appliqué patterns do not include seam allowances.

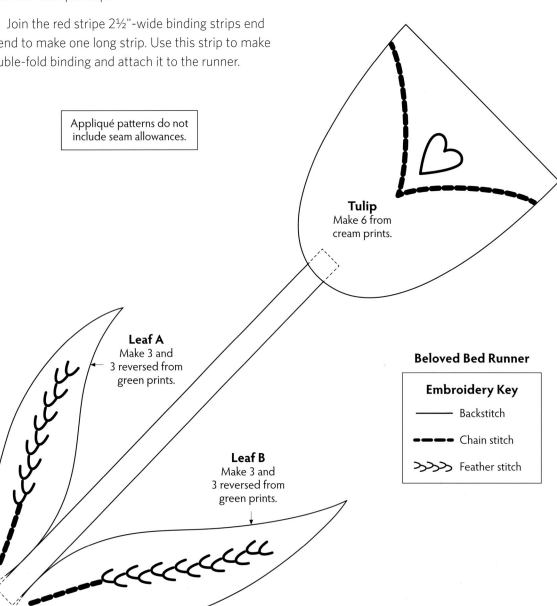

Tulip
Make 6 from cream prints.

Leaf A
Make 3 and 3 reversed from green prints.

Leaf B
Make 3 and 3 reversed from green prints.

Beloved Bed Runner

Embroidery Key	
———	Backstitch
▬ ▬ ▬	Chain stitch
>>>>>	Feather stitch

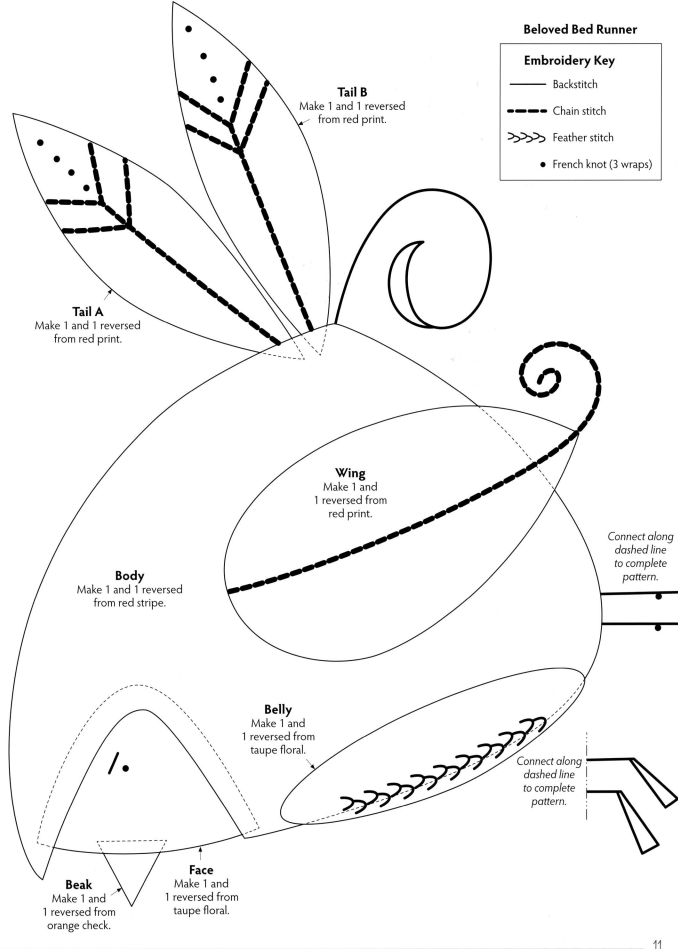

Tail B
Make 1 and 1 reversed
from red print.

Embroidery Key

——	Backstitch
– – –	Chain stitch
>>>>	Feather stitch
•	French knot (3 wraps)

Tail A
Make 1 and 1 reversed
from red print.

Wing
Make 1 and
1 reversed from
red print.

Connect along
dashed line
to complete
pattern.

Body
Make 1 and 1 reversed
from red stripe.

Belly
Make 1 and
1 reversed from
taupe floral.

Connect along
dashed line
to complete
pattern.

Beak
Make 1 and
1 reversed from
orange check.

Face
Make 1 and
1 reversed from
taupe floral.

11

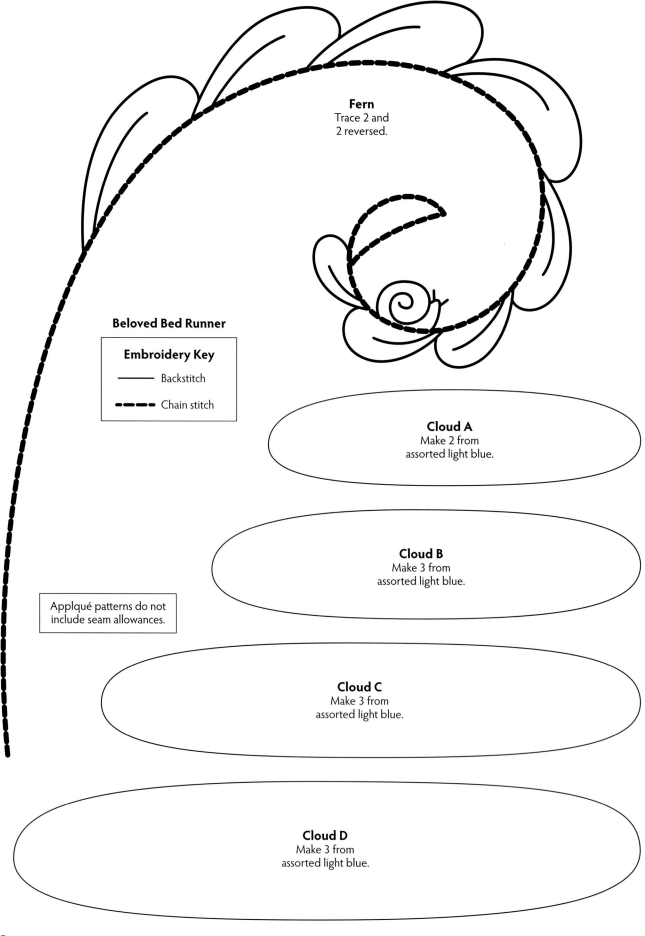

Fern
Trace 2 and
2 reversed.

Beloved Bed Runner

Embroidery Key

—— Backstitch

■■■ Chain stitch

Applqué patterns do not
include seam allowances.

Cloud A
Make 2 from
assorted light blue.

Cloud B
Make 3 from
assorted light blue.

Cloud C
Make 3 from
assorted light blue.

Cloud D
Make 3 from
assorted light blue.

Stitched from the Heart

POCKET FOR YOUR THOUGHTS WALL HANGING

Designed and made by Kori Turner-Goodhart.

 An interactive wall hanging that lets you indulge in sweet and happy handwork, Pocket for Your Thoughts is a perfect gift for someone special who cherishes and keeps little trinkets and notes.

FINISHED WALL HANGING: 16½" × 32½"

MATERIALS

Yardage is based on 42"-wide fabric. Fat quarters measure 18" × 21". Fat eighths measure 9" × 21".

¼ yard *each* of 8 assorted light prints for blocks
⅛ yard *total* of 2 green prints for leaves and stems
1 fat quarter of taupe woven print for pockets
1 fat quarter of taupe solid for pocket linings
1 fat eighth of brown mottled print for flower centers
7 scraps, 6" × 7" *each*, of assorted rose prints
    for flowers
1 scrap, 6" × 7", of yellow print for flower
1½ yards of ½"-wide cotton Cluny lace
¼ yard of fabric for binding
⅞ yard of fabric for backing and hanging sleeve
23" × 39" piece of batting
1 yard of rickrack or decorative trim for hanger
Yardstick trimmed to 21" for hanger
Cosmo Seasons variegated floss in daffodil yellow
    #9004; pink #8008; dark brown #5031; and
    taupe #5028
Eleganza pearl cotton #8 in Marsh Grass #EZM93
Black Pigma Micron pen .01 (fine tip)

4" square of cardstock (optional)
Glue stick (optional)

CUTTING

From *each* of the light prints, cut:
2 squares, 4½" × 4½" (16 total)
8 squares, 2½" × 2½" (64 total)

From *both* of the green prints, cut:
1 strip, ¾" × 20" (2 total)

From the Cluny lace, cut:
8 pieces, 5½" long

From the fabric for binding, cut:
3 strips, 2½" × 42"

From the backing fabric, cut:
1 rectangle, 23" × 39"
1 rectangle, 5" × 15"

FLOSS GUIDE

Use two strands of floss for all stitching unless otherwise noted.

- ✖ **Daffodil yellow:** Petal lines
- ✖ **Dark brown:** Flower center
- ✖ **Marsh Grass:** Leaf swirls and details
- ✖ **Pink:** Petal lines
- ✖ **Taupe:** Pocket details

PIECING THE BLOCKS

Use a ¼" seam allowance. Press the seam allowances as shown by the arrows in the illustrations.

1. Lay out 2½" squares of assorted lights in four rows of four as shown. Join the squares in each row. Join the rows to make a 16 Patch block that measures 8½" square, including seam allowances. Make four 16 Patch blocks.

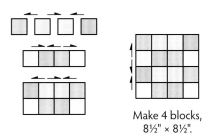

Make 4 blocks,
8½" × 8½".

2. Lay out 4½" squares of assorted lights in two rows of two as shown. Join the squares in each row. Join the rows to make a Four Patch block that measures 8½" square, including seam allowances. Make four Four Patch blocks.

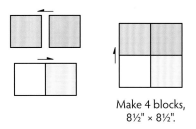

Make 4 blocks,
8½" × 8½".

APPLIQUÉING AND EMBROIDERING THE BLOCKS

The appliqué and embroidery patterns are on page 17. Refer to "Stitch-and-Flip Appliqué" on page 75 for detailed information, or prepare your appliqué shapes for stitching using your favorite method. Refer to "Stitchery and Hand-Embroidery Basics" on page 72 for tracing tips. For specific floss colors, refer to the "Floss Guide" on page 13. Embroidery stitches are diagrammed on pages 73 and 74.

1. Cut and prepare the flower and leaf appliqués as noted on the patterns.

2. Use the green ¾" × 20" strips to make eight stems, ⅜" × 4¾", as shown.

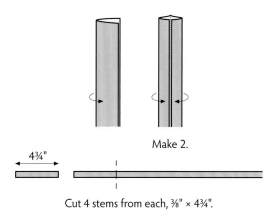

Make 2.

4¾"

Cut 4 stems from each, ⅜" × 4¾".

3. Trace eight pocket shapes onto the wrong side of the taupe solid. With right sides together, layer the taupe solid onto the taupe print. Pin to secure and machine sew directly on the traced lines using the stitch-and-flip method. Turn right side out and press.

4. Attach a 5½" length of lace onto each pocket by machine or hand. Tuck the lace ends to the back of the pocket.

Make 8.

5. Place a prepared flower appliqué on each of the eight blocks. Tuck the top raw end of each stem approximately ½" under the bottom edge of the flower; trim the top of the stem if necessary. Place the pockets on top of the stems. The finished edge of the stem should be at the bottom of the pocket. Add the flower centers and leaves last. Pin or use a glue stick to secure all of the appliqués for stitching.

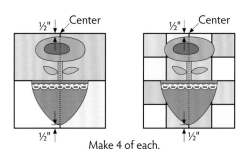

Make 4 of each.

6. Hand appliqué all the pieces to the blocks. Be sure to leave the top edge of the pockets unstitched.

7. Using the Pigma pen, trace the embroidery details (using a light box) onto the block front and appliqués. Work the embroidery to complete the blocks. If needed, cut cardstock in the pocket shape and tuck it into each pocket before embroidering to keep from stitching through to the block background.

8. Once the embroidery is complete, press the blocks from the back and then again from the front.

ASSEMBLING THE WALL HANGING

Lay out the blocks in four rows of two blocks each, alternating the patchwork designs. Sew the blocks together in each row. Join the rows. The wall hanging should measure 16½" × 32½".

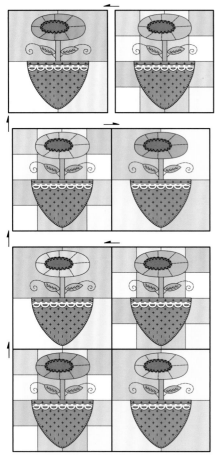

Wall-hanging assembly

FINISHING THE WALL HANGING

For more details on any finishing steps, visit ShopMartingale.com/HowtoQuilt for free, downloadable information.

1. Layer the quilt, batting, and backing. Baste the layers together. Quilt by hand or machine. The wall hanging shown features straight line machine quilting and outline stitching around the appliqués. Trim the excess batting and backing even with the quilt top.

2. To make the hanging sleeve for a yardstick, fold both short ends of the 5" × 15" backing fabric rectangle ½" toward the center, and then fold them in ½" again. Topstitch.

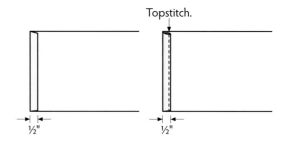

3. Fold the strip in half lengthwise, wrong sides together, and baste the raw edges to the top of the quilt back. The top edge of the sleeve will be secured when the binding is sewn onto the quilt.

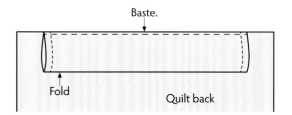

4. Join the 2½"-wide binding strips end to end to make one long strip. Use this strip to make double-fold binding and then attach it to the quilt.

5. Push the bottom edge of the sleeve up just a bit to provide a little give and pin to secure. Blindstitch the bottom of the sleeve in place by hand.

6. Slip the yardstick into the pocket. Tie the rickrack or decorative trim to both ends of the yardstick with a simple knot on each end.

Thought Cards

Thought cards—pretty little notes inscribed with inspirational quotes or personal messages—are a great way to spread joy. Use pretty paper and nice handwriting (or a beautiful font) to personalize cards, then tuck them into this project's pockets as a surprise for the recipient.

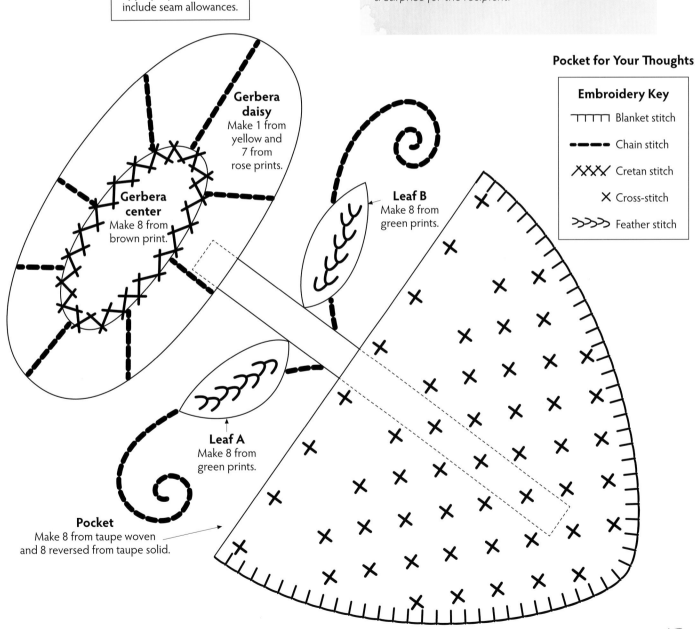

Appliqué patterns do not include seam allowances.

Pocket for Your Thoughts

Embroidery Key	
⊤⊤⊤⊤	Blanket stitch
▬ ▬ ▬	Chain stitch
✗✗✗✗	Cretan stitch
✗	Cross-stitch
⟫⟫⟫⟫	Feather stitch

Gerbera daisy
Make 1 from yellow and 7 from rose prints.

Gerbera center
Make 8 from brown print.

Leaf B
Make 8 from green prints.

Leaf A
Make 8 from green prints.

Pocket
Make 8 from taupe woven and 8 reversed from taupe solid.

BRAVE MOMMA QUILT

Designed and made by Kori Turner-Goodhart. Quilted by Rebecca Silbaugh.

My mom gave me a Brave Momma quilt when I had my sweet daughter, Jaye Anne. I thought it was such a precious idea that I had to design my own version to share with you. This quilt has incredible hand-appliqué and embroidery details yet is surprisingly fast to whip up!

FINISHED QUILT: 58½" × 68½"

MATERIALS

Yardage is based on 42"-wide fabric. Fat eighths measure 9" × 21".

2⅝ yards of gray linen for left side panel and embroidery background

⅜ yard *each* of 5 assorted pink florals (#1–#5) for pinwheels and checkerboard

⅞ yard of cream print for patchwork strips*

5 fat eighths of assorted prints (red, yellow, green, orange, and pink) for appliqués

1 fat eighth of blue print for pinwheel and appliqués

1 fat eighth of purple print for pinwheel and appliqués

¾" × 20" strip of charcoal print for pinwheel sticks

⅝ yard of gray stripe for binding

4¼ yards of fabric for backing

65" × 75" piece of batting

2 skeins of Cosmo solid floss in charcoal #895

Black Pigma Micron pen .01 (fine tip)

Glue stick (optional)

*If your cream print is less than 40½" wide after removing selvages, you'll need 1⅛ yards.

CUTTING

From the cream print, cut:
2 rectangles, 6½" × 40½"
2 rectangles, 6½" × 16½"
1 rectangle, 6½" × 12½"
1 rectangle, 8½" × 16½"

From the gray linen, cut:
1 rectangle on the *lengthwise* grain, 30½" × 68½"
1 square, 16½" × 16½"

From *each of* pink florals #3 and #4, cut:
10 squares, 4½" × 4½" (20 total)
2 squares, 2⅞" × 2⅞" (4 total)

From *each of* pink florals #1, #2, and #5, cut:
10 squares, 4½" × 4½" (30 total)

From *each of* the blue and purple fat eighths, cut:
2 squares, 2⅞" × 2⅞" (4 total)

From the gray stripe, cut:
7 strips, 2½" × 42"

Stitched from the Heart

PIECING THE PINWHEEL BLOCKS

Use a ¼" seam allowance. Press the seam allowances as shown by the arrows in the illustrations.

1. Use a pencil to mark a diagonal line from corner to corner on a pink #4 square and layer it on top of a blue 2⅞" square, right sides together. Sew ¼" from each side of the drawn line. Cut on the line to yield two half-square-triangle units that measure 2½" square, including seam allowances. Trim off the dog-ears. Make four units. Repeat with the pink #3 and purple 2⅞" squares to make four units.

Make 4 of each unit,
2½" × 2½".

2. Lay out the blue half-square-triangle units in two rows of two as shown. Join the pieces in each row. Join the rows to make a Pinwheel block that measures 4½" square, including seam allowances. Repeat with the purple units to make a second Pinwheel block.

Make 1 of each block,
4½" × 4½".

ARRANGING PATCHWORK PANELS

1. To arrange the top panel, lay out 40 of the pink 4½" squares in numerical order from left to right and top to bottom in 10 rows of four squares as shown below. In row 5, insert the blue Pinwheel block in place of pink #4 and continue in numerical order so that row 10 ends with a print #5 square.

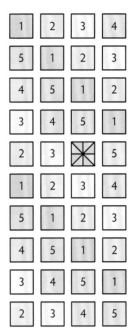

Top panel layout

2. For the bottom panel, lay out the 11 remaining pink 4½" squares in three rows of four, beginning with the purple Pinwheel block made with pink #3 and continuing in numerical order. *Do not* join the squares yet.

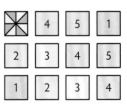

Bottom panel layout

ADDING THE APPLIQUÉ

The appliqué patterns are on page 26. Refer to "Stitch-and-Flip Appliqué" on page 75 for detailed information, or prepare appliqué shapes for stitching using your favorite method.

1. Cut and prepare the following appliqués:

✄ **12 circles:** 2 red, 2 orange, 3 yellow, 2 green, 1 blue, 1 purple, and 1 pink.

✄ **4 hearts:** 1 red, 1 orange, 1 green, and 1 pink

2. Pin or glue baste the prepared circle and heart appliqués on 16 of the assorted pink 4½" squares in the quilt layout, using the photo on page 20 as a guide. Hand appliqué the circles and hearts to the 4½" squares and replace the squares in the layout.

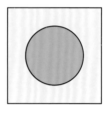

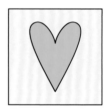

Make 12. Make 4.

3. Fold down one end of the charcoal ¾" × 20" strip by ⅜". Fold each long edge to the vertical center and press. Crosscut the strip to make two sticks, ⅜" × 9".

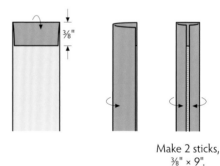

Make 2 sticks,
⅜" × 9".

4. Join the squares in each row in the top panel and then join the rows. The top panel should measure 16½" × 40½", including seam allowances. Repeat for the bottom panel, which should measure 12½" × 16½", including seam allowances.

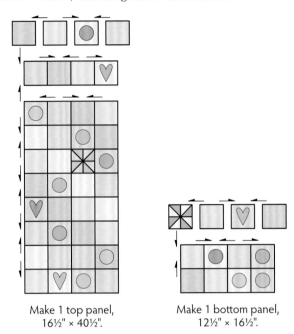

Make 1 top panel,
16½" × 40½".

Make 1 bottom panel,
12½" × 16½".

5. Lay out a stick from step 3 below the blue Pinwheel block so the finished edge aligns with the bottom of the block. With a seam ripper, carefully make a ½" opening in the center of the join between the third squares of rows 7 and 8. Insert the raw end of the pinwheel stick into the opening. Pin or glue baste the stick in place and stitch the opening closed.

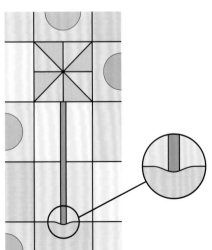

6. Pin or glue baste a second stick under the purple Pinwheel block with the finished edge aligned with the bottom of the block; the raw edge will be caught in the binding. Hand appliqué the sticks to the quilt. Press flat when the appliqué is complete.

ADDING THE EMBROIDERY

The embroidery patterns are on pages 26–29. Refer to "Stitchery and Hand-Embroidery Basics" on page 72 for tracing tips. Embroidery stitches are diagrammed on page 73 and 74.

1. Following the embroidery guide, feather stitch all around the Pinwheel seams and fly stitch down the length of the stems using two strands of charcoal floss.

2. Decide which inspirational quote you'd like to use (see "What Is Momma Having?" on page 21 and the patterns on pages 26–29). Draw a 12" square frame in the center of the gray linen 16½" square, and then trace the quote pattern in the center. Trace the bird embroidery pattern onto the cream 8½" × 16½" rectangle, making sure the large bird is placed exactly 1¼" from the bottom of the rectangle.

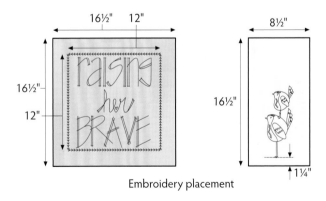

Embroidery placement

3. Hand embroider the designs using three strands of charcoal floss and the fly stitch for the frame, four strands for the lettering, and two strands for the bird. When complete, trim the sides of the bird unit so that it measures 6½" wide, making sure to keep the embroidery centered. Trim no more than ½" from the bottom of the rectangle and the remainder from the top so that it measures 12½" long. Press flat.

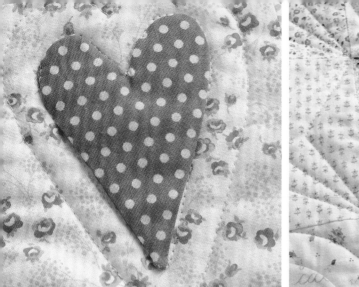

ASSEMBLING THE QUILT TOP

1. Join the top patchwork panel, the embroidered panel, and the bottom patchwork panel. The unit should measure 16½" × 68½", including seam allowances.

2. Join the cream rectangles as shown to create two long strips of three rectangles each; note that the right unit includes the embroidered bird rectangle. Each strip should measure 6½" × 68½" each, including seam allowances.

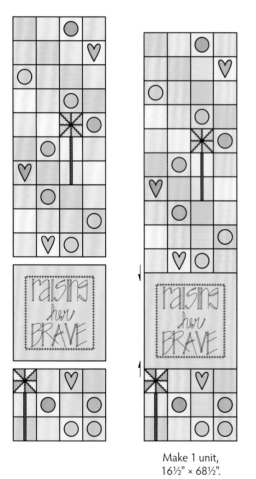

Make 1 unit,
16½" × 68½".

6½"
×
40½"

6½"
×
16½"

6½"
×
12½"

Make 1 of each,
6½" × 68½".

3. Join the embroidered cream strip to the right edge of the checkerboard unit and the remaining strip to the left. The unit should measure 28½" × 68½", including seam allowances.

4. Sew the gray linen 30½" × 68½" rectangle to the left side of the pieced unit as shown below. The quilt top should measure 58½" × 68½".

DON'T BITE YOUR NAILS!

I like a .01 Pigma Micron pen to mark embroidery designs onto fabric, but if permanent ink worries you, try a washable marker or FriXion pen, which is removed with the heat of an iron. Trust me, I understand you want that swirl to be perfect. Just make sure that what you choose has a fine tip for marking accurate embroidery lines.

FINISHING THE QUILT

For more details on any finishing steps, visit ShopMartingale.com/HowtoQuilt for free, downloadable information.

1. Layer the quilt top, batting, and backing together. Quilt by hand or machine. The quilt shown is machine quilted with modern swirls, geometric patterns, and feathers. The appliqués are outline quilted. Trim the excess batting and backing even with the quilt top.

2. Join the gray stripe 2½"-wide strips end to end to make one long strip. Use this strip to make double-fold binding and attach it to the quilt.

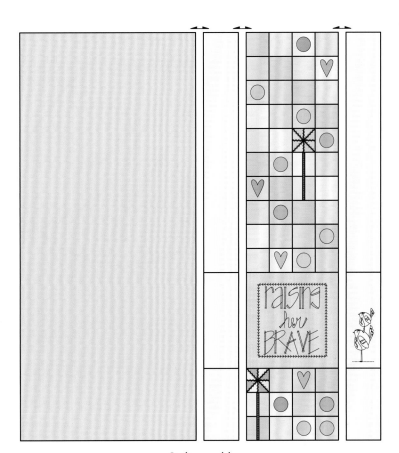

Quilt assembly

Appliqué patterns do not include seam allowances.

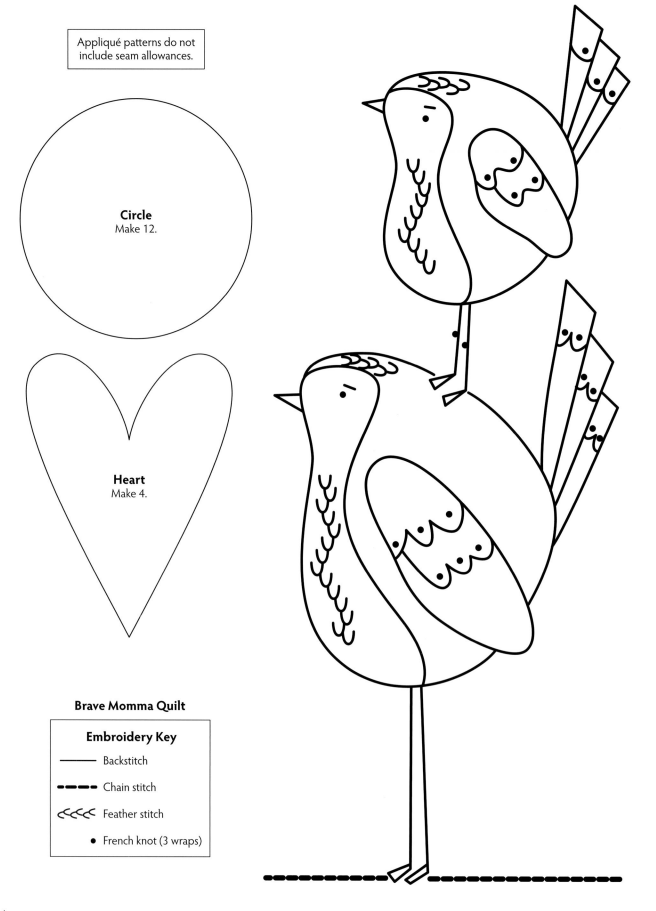

Circle
Make 12.

Heart
Make 4.

Brave Momma Quilt

Embroidery Key

——— Backstitch

▬ ▬ ▬ Chain stitch

‹‹‹‹ Feather stitch

● French knot (3 wraps)

Stitched from the Heart

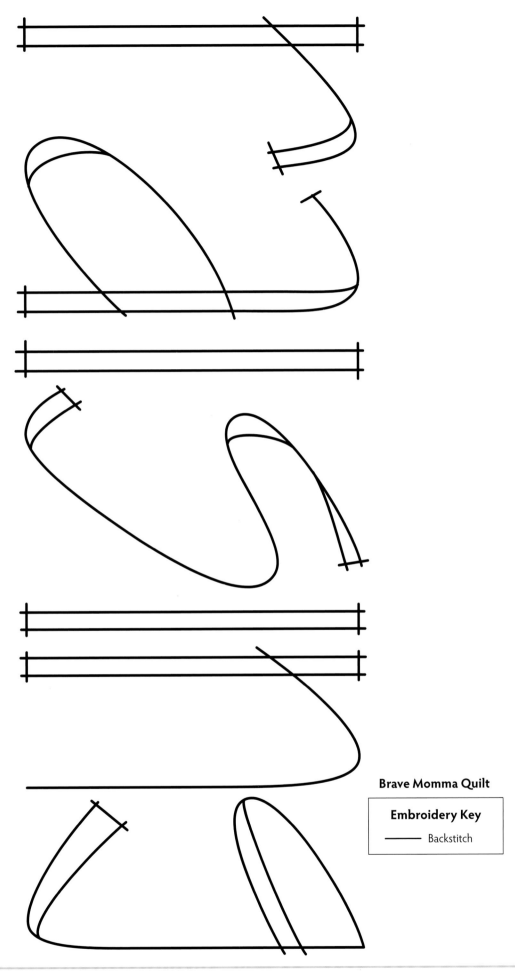

Brave Momma Quilt

Embroidery Key

— Backstitch

Stitched from the Heart

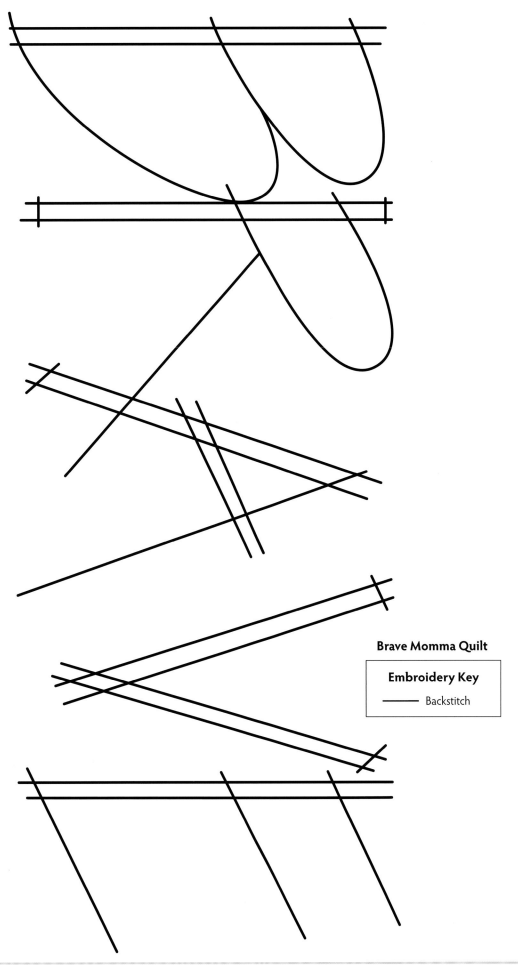

Brave Momma Quilt

Embroidery Key
—— Backstitch

BRAVE LITTLE LOVE QUILT

Designed and made by Kori Turner-Goodhart. Quilted by Rebecca Silbaugh.

Brave mommas should teach their little loves that they, too, are brave. A companion to the Brave Momma Quilt (page 19), this sweet quilt is made with simple patchwork, hand embroidery, and appliqué details from the heart.

FINISHED QUILT: 32½" × 36½"

MATERIALS

Yardage is based on 42"-wide fabric. Fat eighths measure 9" × 21".

1 yard of pink floral for left side panel, brave patch, and appliqué
½ yard of gray linen for patchwork
7 fat eighths (or scraps) of assorted prints (red, orange, yellow, blue, green, pink, and purple) for patchwork and pinwheel
2 scraps, at least 6" × 8" *each,* of different white prints for pinwheel and appliqués
½" × 7" strip of charcoal print for pinwheel stick
⅓ yard of gray stripe for binding
1¼ yards of fabric for backing
39" × 43" piece of batting
1 skein of Cosmo solid floss in charcoal #895
Black Pigma Micron pen .01 (fine tip)
Glue stick

CUTTING

From the pink floral, cut:
1 rectangle, 17½" × 36½"
1 square, 11½" × 11½"

From the gray linen, cut:
2 rectangles, 3½" × 18½"
3 rectangles, 3½" × 9½"
1 rectangle, 5½" × 11½"

From the assorted prints, cut a *total* of:
26 squares, 3½" × 3½"

From the pink fat eighth, cut:
2 squares, 2⅜" × 2⅜"

From 1 white print scrap, cut:
2 squares, 2⅜" × 2⅜"

From the gray stripe, cut:
4 strips, 2½" × 42"

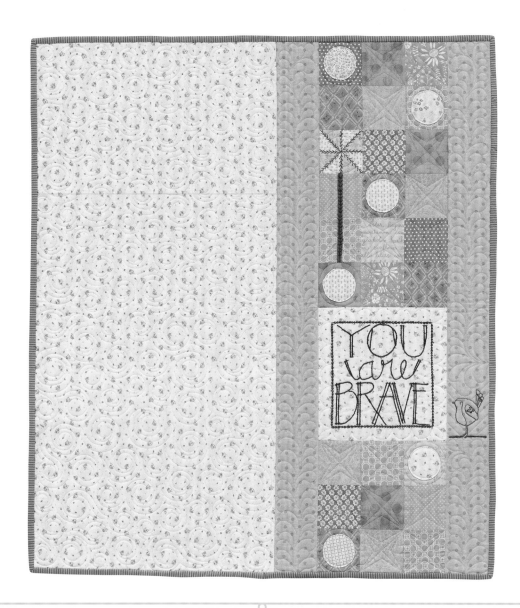

Piecing the Pinwheel Unit

Use a ¼" seam allowance. Press as shown by the arrows in the illustrations.

1. Use a pencil to mark a diagonal line from corner to corner on a white 2⅜" square and layer it on top of a pink 2⅜" square, right sides together. Sew ¼" from each side of the drawn line. Cut on the line to yield two half-square-triangle units each measuring 2" square, including seam allowances. Trim off the dog-ears. Repeat to make four units.

Make 4 total,
2" × 2".

2. Lay out the half-square-triangle units in two rows of two to make a pinwheel. Join the pieces in each row. Join the rows to complete the Pinwheel block. The block should measure 3½" square, including seam allowances.

Make 1 block,
3½" × 3½".

Stitched from the Heart

3. Lay out the Pinwheel block, one yellow 3½" square, and one purple 3½" square in a vertical row as shown. Join the pieces to complete the pinwheel unit. The unit should measure 3½" × 9½".

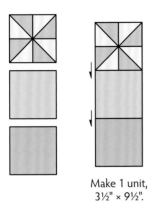

Make 1 unit,
3½" × 9½".

4. Lay out the pinwheel stick on the pinwheel unit, with the finished short edge of the stick aligned with the bottom of the Pinwheel block. Hand appliqué the stick to the pinwheel unit and trim the bottom end of the stick even with the bottom of the unit. Press flat.

Make 1.

ADDING THE APPLIQUÉ

The appliqué pattern is on page 35. Refer to "Stitch-and-Flip Appliqué" on page 75 for detailed information, or prepare your appliqué shapes for stitching using your favorite method. 1. Cut and prepare six circles using the white scraps and pink floral.

2. Pin or glue the prepared circle appliqués onto six of the assorted 3½" squares. Hand appliqué the circles to the squares and press flat.

Make 6 in
assorted colors.

3. Fold under ½" at one end of the charcoal ½" × 7" strip. Fold both long edges to the vertical center and press to make a ¼"-wide pinwheel stick.

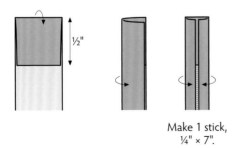

½"

Make 1 stick,
¼" × 7".

ADDING THE EMBROIDERY

The embroidery patterns are on pages 35 and 36. Refer to "Stitchery and Hand-Embroidery Basics" on page 72 for tracing tips. Embroidery stitches are diagrammed on pages 73 and 74.

1. Following the embroidery guide, feather stitch the Pinwheel seams and fly stitch along the length of the stem using two strands of charcoal floss.

2. Draw a 7" square frame in the center of the pink floral 11½" square, and then trace the quote pattern from page 36 in the center. Trace the bird pattern from page 35 onto the gray linen 5½" × 11½" rectangle, making sure the bird is placed exactly 1¼" from the bottom of the rectangle.

3. Hand embroider the designs using two strands of charcoal floss for the bird and three strands for the lettering. When complete, trim equal amounts from the left and right edges of the bird unit so that it measures 3½" wide; make sure to center the embroidery. Trim no more than ½" from the bottom of the rectangle and the remainder from the top so that it measures 9½" long. Trim the 11½" square to 9½" square, centering the framed lettering. Press both pieces flat.

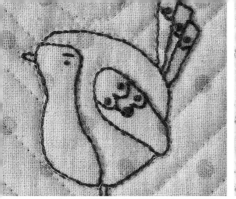

ASSEMBLING THE QUILT TOP

1. Lay out two appliquéd squares and four assorted 3½" squares in three vertical rows of two squares each. Sew the pieces together in each row. Join the rows to make unit A. Unit A should measure 6½" × 9½", including seam allowances.

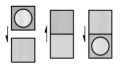

Unit A,
6½" × 9½".

2. Lay out the pinwheel unit, an appliquéd square, and five assorted 3½" squares in three vertical rows. Sew the pieces together in each row. Join the rows to make unit B. Unit B should measure 9½" square, including seam allowances.

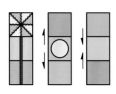

Unit B,
9½" × 9½".

3. Join an appliquéd square and two assorted 3½" squares in a row to make unit C. Unit C should measure 3½" × 9½", including seam allowances.

Unit C,
3½" × 9½".

4. Lay out two appliquéd squares and seven assorted 3½" squares in three rows of three. Sew the pieces together in each row. Join the rows to make unit D. Unit D should measure 9½" square, including seam allowances.

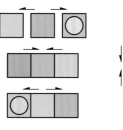

Unit D,
9½" × 9½".

5. Join units A–D and the embroidered quote unit as shown to complete the checkerboard unit that measures 9½" × 36½", including seam allowances.

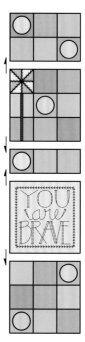

Make 1 unit,
9½" × 36½".

6. Lay out the gray linen rectangles as shown to create two long strips of three rectangles each; note that the right unit includes the embroidered bird rectangle. Sew together into two strips that measure 3½" × 36½" each, including seam allowances.

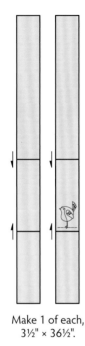

Make 1 of each,
3½" × 36½".

7. Join the strips to opposite sides of the checkerboard unit. The unit should now measure 15½" × 36½", including seam allowances.

8. Join the pink floral 17½" × 36½" rectangle to the left side of the unit. The quilt top should measure 32½" × 36½".

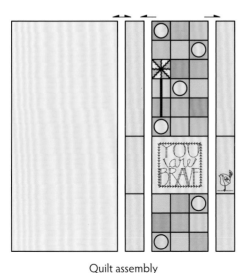

Quilt assembly

FINISHING THE QUILT

For more details on any finishing steps, visit ShopMartingale.com/HowtoQuilt for free, downloadable information.

1. Layer the quilt top, batting, and backing. Quilt by hand or machine. The quilt shown is machine quilted with modern swirls, geometric patterns, and feathers. The appliqués are outline quilted. Trim the excess batting and backing even with the quilt top.

2. Join the gray stripe 2½"-wide strips end to end to make one long strip. Use this strip to make double-fold binding and then attach it to the quilt.

Appliqué pattern does not include seam allowance.

Circle
Make 6.

Brave Little Love Quilt

Embroidery Key

——— Backstitch

– – – – Chain stitch

• French knot (3 wraps)

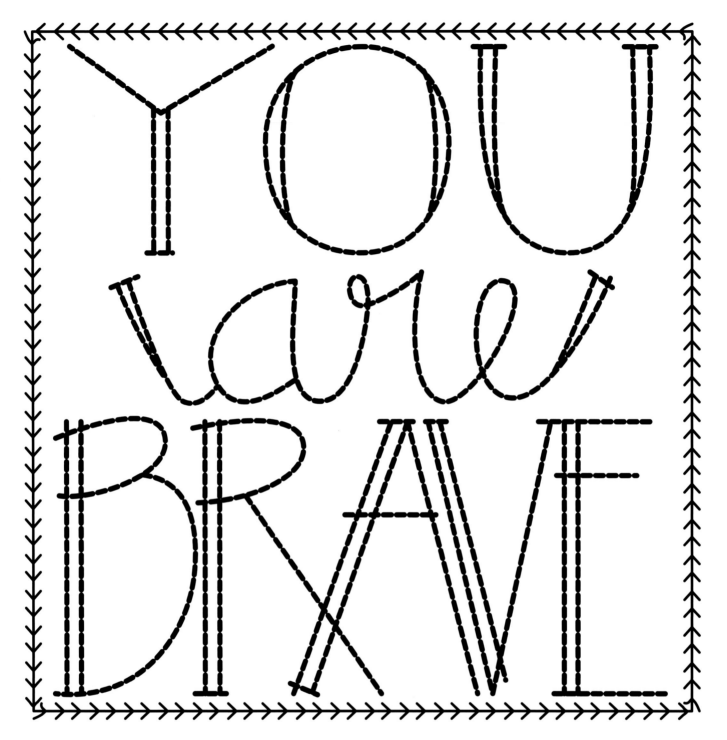

Brave Little Love Quilt

Embroidery Key

▬ ▬ ▬ Chain stitch

≫≫≫≫≫ Fly stitch

Stitched from the Heart

LITTLE PREZZIES FROM THE HEART MUG RUG AND PINCUSHION

Designed and made by Kori Turner-Goodhart.

The best gifts are the ones that are unexpected. Once I made one mug rug and pincushion pair, I couldn't stop. I made a variety of them in different color palettes and with assorted embroidered affirmations for my friends. Charming mug rugs and pincushions make the perfect gifts for all your stitching friends.

FINISHED MUG RUG OR PINCUSHION: 6½" × 8½"

MATERIALS

Materials yield 1 pincushion and 1 mug rug. Yardage is based on 42"-wide fabric. Fat eighths measure 9" × 21".

2 scraps, at least 4" × 4" *each*, of fabric for four-patch units
1 scrap, at least 6" × 6", of fabric for rectangles
2 scraps, at least 8" × 11" *each*, of fabric for strips
1 fat eighth of fabric for backing
1½" × 42" strip of fabric for mug-rug binding
1 fat eighth of muslin for pincushion lining
8" × 10" piece of batting for mug rug
Assorted trims and buttons for embellishing
Assorted threads for embroidery to match your color palette
Ground walnut shells for pincushion stuffing
Black Pigma Micron pen .01 (fine tip)

CUTTING

From *each* 4" × 4" scrap, cut:
4 squares, 1½" × 1½" (8 total)

From the 6" × 6" scrap, cut:
2 rectangles, 2½" × 4½"

From *each* 8" × 11" scrap, cut:
6 strips, 1½" × 6½" (12 total)

From the backing, cut:
1 rectangle, 6½" × 8½"
1 rectangle, 8" × 10"

From the muslin, cut:
2 rectangles, 6½" × 8½"

SHARE YOUR PREZZIES!

Post your Little Prezzies from the Heart on social media using the following hashtags: #littleprezziesfromtheheartpincushion #littleprezziesfromtheheartmugrug #olivegracestudios #stitchedfromtheheartbook

PIECING THE BLOCKS

Use a ¼" seam allowance. Press the seam allowances as shown by the arrows in the illustrations.

1. Lay out the 1½" squares in two rows of two, alternating the fabrics. Sew the squares together in each row. Sew the rows together to make a four-patch unit that measures 2½" square. Make two.

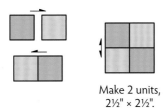

Make 2 units,
2½" × 2½".

2. Join a 2½" × 4½" rectangle to the left side of a four-patch unit. The unit should now measure 2½" × 6½". Make two.

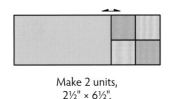

Make 2 units,
2½" × 6½".

3. Join four 1½" × 6½" strips, alternating the fabrics, to make a unit that measures 4½" × 6½". Make two. Join two 1½" × 6½" strips to make a unit that measures 2½" × 6½". Make two.

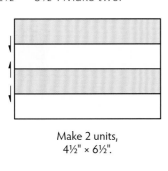

Make 2 units,
4½" × 6½".

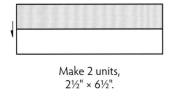

Make 2 units,
2½" × 6½".

4. Lay out a unit from step 2 and two different units from step 3 in three rows. Note that I used slightly different arrangements for the two blocks. Join the rows to make a block. Repeat to make two blocks that measure 6½" × 8½", including seam allowances.

Mug rug,
6½" × 8½".

Pincushion,
6½" × 8½".

ADDING THE EMBROIDERY

The embroidery patterns are on page 41. Refer to "Stitchery and Hand-Embroidery Basics" on page 72 for tracing tips. Embroidery stitches are diagrammed on pages 73 and 74.

1. Mark and stitch the embroidery details on both blocks. Use your favorite stitches and two strands of floss. Have fun! Personalize your gift using the ½" alphabet patterns on page 79.

2. Press both blocks flat. Sew on buttons, lace, ribbons, or other embellishments as desired.

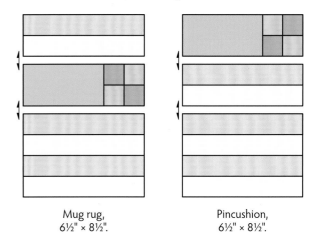

GRANDMA'S BUTTON BOX

Embellish your pincushion and mug rugs with buttons, ribbon, or even lace. This is a great way to pass on family treasures.

Little Prezzies from the Heart Mug Rug and Pincushion

2. Pin and then sew around the perimeter, leaving a 3" opening at the bottom of the pincushion for turning and stuffing. Snip off the seam allowances at all four corners as shown.

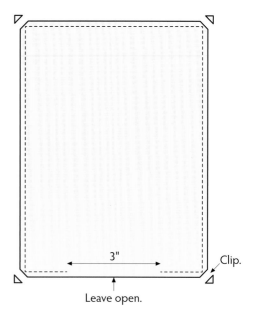

3"

Clip.

Leave open.

3. Turn the pincushion right side out through the opening. Carefully push out the corners. Press, then fill the pincushion with the crushed walnut shells in between the two muslin layers. Hand stitch the opening closed. For an extra detail, embroider a feather stitch on top of the blind stitch that you used to close the pincushion.

ASSEMBLING THE PINCUSHION

1. Choose a block for the pincushion. With right sides together, layer it on the 6½" × 8½" backing rectangle. Layer the two muslin rectangles on top of the layered front and back.

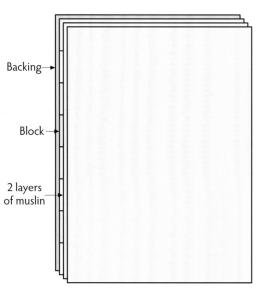

Backing →

Block →

2 layers of muslin →

ASSEMBLING THE MUG RUG

1. Layer the remaining block on top of the batting and the 8" × 10" piece of backing fabric to make a mini-quilt.

2. Quilt the mug rug as desired. I machine quilted approximately ¼" on both sides of the strip seams and then inside the squares and rectangle.

3. Trim the excess batting and backing even with the mug-rug top.

4. Use the 1½" × 42" strip to make single-fold binding and attach it to the mug rug.

Stitched from the Heart

DREAMS DO COME *true*

KEEP ~~going~~ YOU ARE WORTH it

MAKE YOUR OWN *Luck*

YOU ARE SO *Loved*

One DAY *at* A TIME

**Little Prezzies from the Heart
Mug Rug and Pincushion**

Embroidery Key
—————— Backstitch
━ ━ ━ ━ Chain stitch
● French knot (4 wraps)

Little Prezzies from the Heart Mug Rug and Pincushion

HEART OF THE FAMILY BANNER

Designed and made by Kori Turner-Goodhart.

 Inspired by a family tree but with more sentiment, personalized banners will be the hit of the family reunion. Add family names and a heart for each family member. You can even leave space for later additions. Embroidery and crazy-patch hearts overload these beauties with charm.

FINISHED BANNER: 12½" × 36½"

MATERIALS

Yardage is based on 42"-wide fabric. Fat eighths measure 9" × 21".

3 fat eighths of assorted light gray prints for patchwork (light gray prints #1, #2, and #3)
¼ yard of light gray print #4 for background
2½" × 36½" strip of light gray print #5 for embroidery background
3½" × 13½" strip of light gray print #6 for embroidery background
5½" × 15½" strip of light gray print #7 for embroidery background
Assorted scrap rectangles, 2⅞" × 3¾" each, for appliqués*
Assorted scraps for back of appliqués**

See "The Crazy Heart Formula" on page 45 to estimate how many scraps you'll need.

**If you're using the stitch-and-flip method.*

¼ yard of dark gray print for border
⅓ yard of gray stripe for binding
¼ yard of fabric for backing
18" × 43" piece of batting
Cosmo solid floss in charcoal #895
Cosmo variegated floss in cardinal red #5005
Dazzle thread in Frost Green #6108
Eleganza pearl cotton #8 in Carbon #EZM04
Black Pigma Micron pen .01 (fine tip)
Glue stick (optional)

CUTTING

From light gray print #1, cut:
3 strips, 1½" × 21"

From light gray print #2, cut:
3 strips, 1½" × 21"

From light gray print #3, cut:
3 rectangles, 2½" × 3½"

From light gray print #4, cut:
1 strip, 3½" × 12½"
1 rectangle, 5½" × 10½"

From the dark gray print, cut:
2 strips, 1½" × 36½"
2 rectangles, 1½" × 5½"
2 rectangles, 1½" × 3½"

From the gray stripe, cut:
4 strips, 2½" × 42"

FLOSS GUIDE

Use three strands of floss for all stitching unless otherwise noted. For the Crazy hearts, use assorted stitches and thread colors for the embroidery so that each heart is different.

- ✖ **Charcoal:** Crazy hearts, lettering
- ✖ **Cardinal red:** Crazy hearts
- ✖ **Frost Green:** Crazy hearts
- ✖ **Carbon:** Crazy hearts, letter accents

PIECING THE BACKGROUND

Use a ¼" seam allowance. Press the seam allowances as shown by the arrows in the illustrations.

1. Join the light gray #1 and #2 strips into two strip sets, alternating the fabrics. Crosscut strip set A into 12 segments, 1½" × 3½". Crosscut strip set B into six segments, 1½" × 3½".

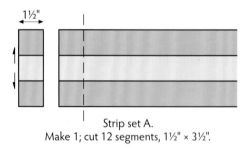

Strip set A.
Make 1; cut 12 segments, 1½" × 3½".

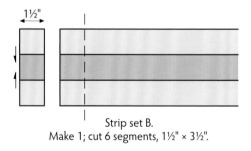

Strip set B.
Make 1; cut 6 segments, 1½" × 3½".

2. Join three strip-set segments to make a Nine Patch block that measures 3½" square, including seam allowances. Repeat to make six Nine Patch blocks.

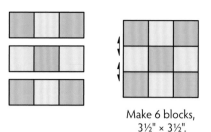

Make 6 blocks,
3½" × 3½".

3. Lay out the two dark gray 1½" × 3½" rectangles, three Nine Patch blocks, the light gray #6 strip, and the light gray #4 strip in a row as shown. Sew the pieces together. The row should measure 3½" × 36½", including seam allowances.

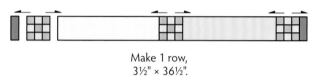

Make 1 row,
3½" × 36½".

4. Sew a light gray #3 rectangle to the top of each remaining Nine Patch block. Make three units. Join the units in a row, inverting the center unit as shown to make a unit that measures 5½" × 9½", including seam allowances.

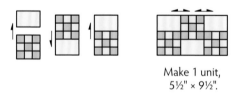

Make 1 unit,
5½" × 9½".

5. Lay out the two dark gray 1½" × 5½" rectangles, the light gray #4 rectangle, the unit from step 4, and the light gray #7 rectangle in a row as shown. Join the units to make a row that measures 5½" × 36½", including seam allowances.

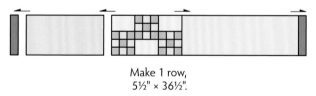

Make 1 row,
5½" × 36½".

6. Sew a dark gray 1½" × 36½" strip to the top of the unit from step 3 and a dark gray 1½" × 36½" strip to the bottom of the unit from step 5. Join the two units to the light gray print #5 strip to make a banner that measures 12½" × 36½".

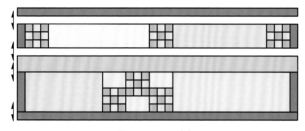

Banner assembly

MAKING THE CRAZY HEARTS

Choose the number and sizes of Crazy hearts you'd like to include on your banner. My banner uses two large hearts, three medium hearts, and one small heart. Referring to "The Crazy Heart Formula" at right, piece the assorted scrap rectangles into patchwork. Press the seam allowances open to allow for easier tracing and flatter appliqué.

THE CRAZY HEART FORMULA

Use this formula to estimate the number of scrap rectangles you'll need to make the Crazy hearts.

To make two large Crazy hearts, you'll need a 7" × 10" piece of patchwork (eight assorted 2⅞" × 3¾" rectangles).

To make three medium Crazy hearts, you'll need a 7" × 10" piece of patchwork (eight assorted 2⅞" × 3¾" rectangles).

To make one small Crazy heart, you'll need a 5" × 7" piece of patchwork (four assorted 2¾" × 3¾" rectangles).

You'll also need a same-sized scrap of fabric for the back of each patchwork piece for stitch-and-flip appliqué.

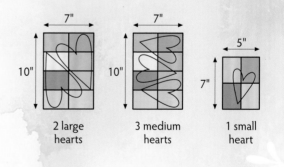

2 large hearts   3 medium hearts   1 small heart

Heart of the Family Banner

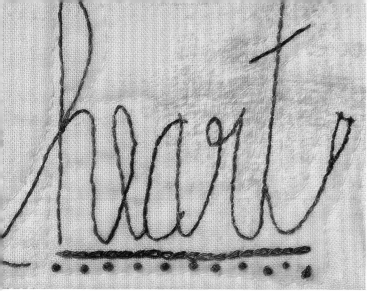

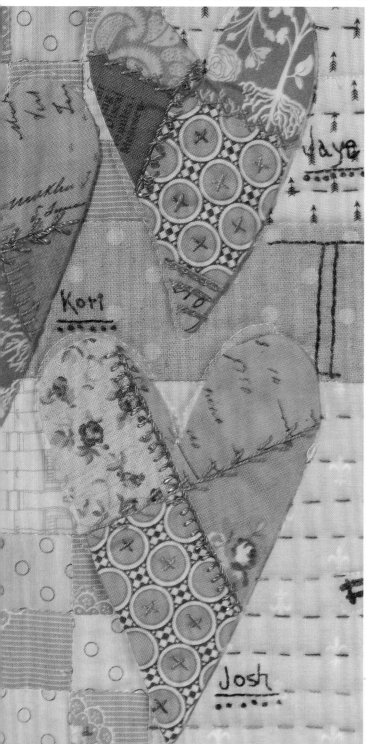

APPLIQUÉING AND EMBROIDERING THE BANNER

The appliqué patterns are on page 49. The embroidery patterns are on pages 47 and 48. Refer to "Stitch-and-Flip Appliqué" on page 75 for detailed information, or prepare your appliqué shapes for stitching using your favorite method. Refer to "Stitchery and Hand-Embroidery Basics" on page 72 for tracing tips. For specific floss colors, refer to the "Floss Guide" on page 44. Embroidery stitches are diagrammed on pages 73 and 74.

1. Cut and prepare your desired number of hearts from the prepared patchwork. When tracing the heart patterns onto the blocks, be sure to angle them to achieve the look of an old-fashioned crazy quilt.

2. Lay out the prepared appliqués on the pieced background. Play with the arrangement of hearts until you're happy with the placement, which may or may not match mine. Pin or use a glue stick to secure the appliqués.

3. Hand appliqué the pieces to the background and press flat.

4. Mark and stitch the letters and embroidery details onto the banner background and appliqués using the patterns on pages 47 and 48. To customize your names or wording, use the 2" alphabet patterns on pages 77 and 78. To include first names next to the patchwork hearts, use your own handwriting or the ½" alphabet on page 79. Underline with a backstitch and a series of French knots as shown.

5. Press the completed embroidery.

SHARE YOUR FAMILY'S HEART!

*Post your Heart of the Family Banner on social media using the following hashtags:
#heartofthefamilybanner #olivegracestudios
#stitchedfromtheheartbook #martingaletpp*

CRAZY HEARTS

To lend the banner a vintage feel, I embroidered the hearts with a variety of stitches in different threads. See "Embroidery Stitches" on pages 73–74 for ideas.

FINISHING THE BANNER

For more details on any finishing steps, visit ShopMartingale.com/HowtoQuilt for free, downloadable information.

1. Layer the banner top, batting, and backing and baste the layers together. Quilt by hand or machine. The yard-long art features big-stitch hand quilting combined with in-the-ditch machine stitching and horizontal lines. Trim the excess batting and backing even with the quilt top.

2. Join the gray stripe 2½"-wide strips end to end to make one long strip. Use this strip to make double-fold binding and use it to bind the banner.

Heart of the Family Banner

Embroidery Key	
——	Backstitch
▪▪▪▪▪	Chain stitch
●	French knot (2 wraps)

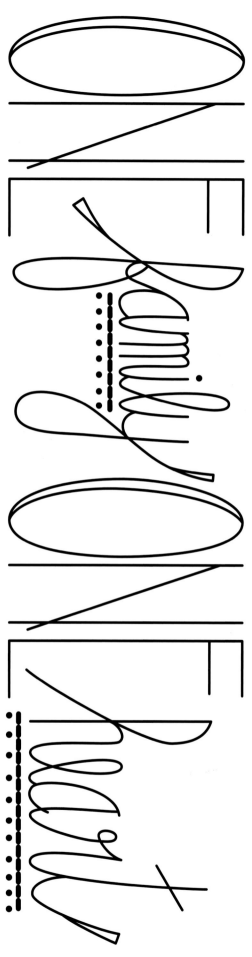

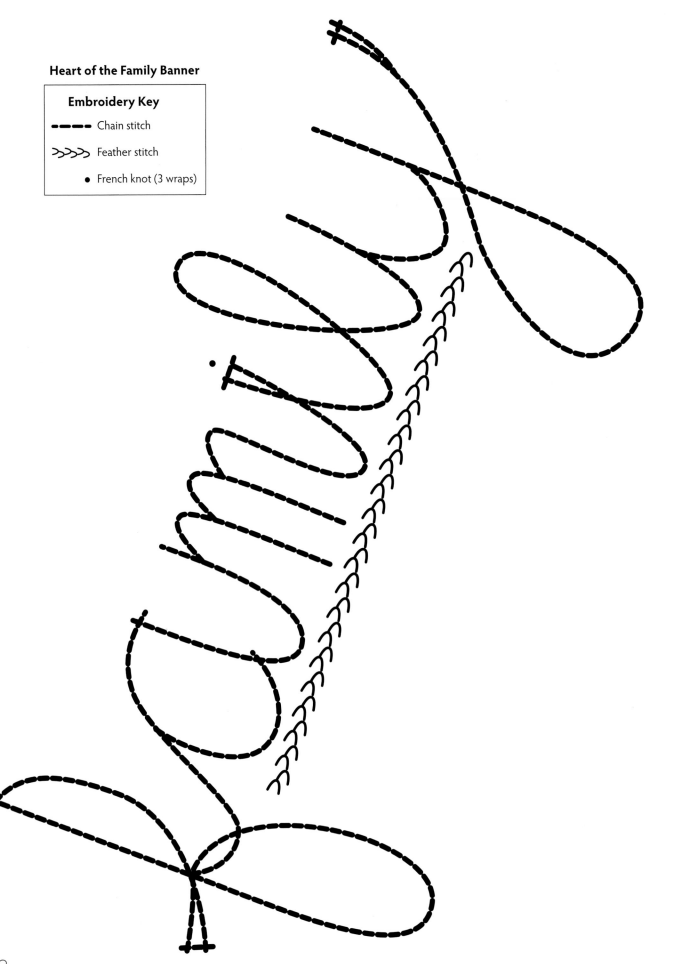

Heart of the Family Banner

Embroidery Key

- – – – Chain stitch
- >>>>> Feather stitch
- • French knot (3 wraps)

Stitched from the Heart

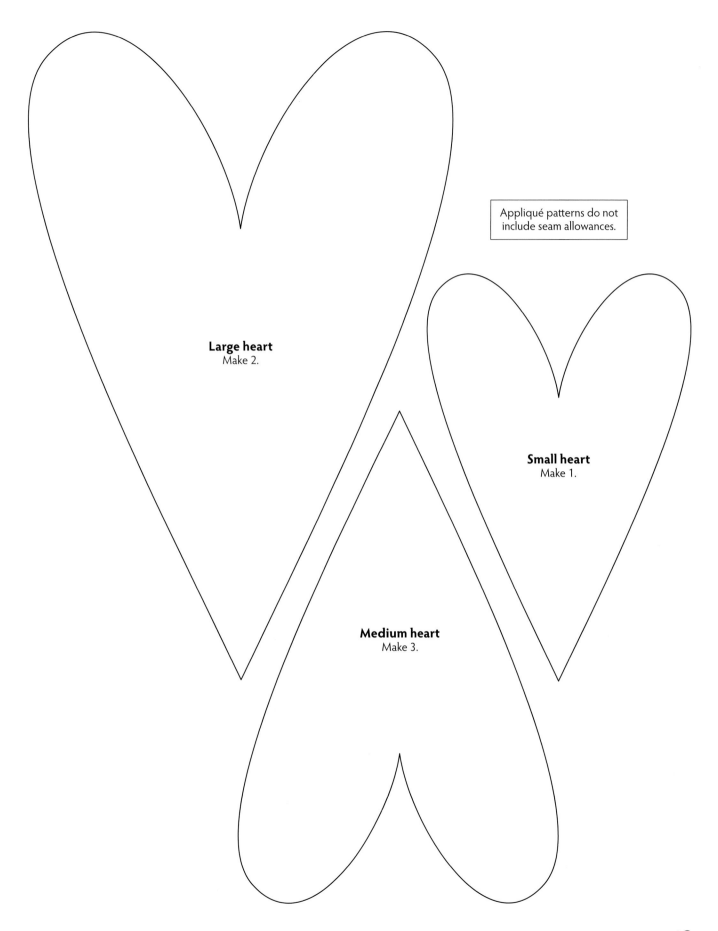

Appliqué patterns do not
include seam allowances.

Large heart
Make 2.

Small heart
Make 1.

Medium heart
Make 3.

Heart of the Family Banner

SIGNED WITH LOVE AUTOGRAPH QUILT

Designed and made by Kori Turner-Goodhart. Quilted by Linda Sekerak.

 A modern update on a traditional autograph quilt, *Signed with Love* is a sentimental heirloom to be cherished for generations to come. Loved ones can handwrite messages from the heart in these simple, customizable pieced blocks.

FINISHED QUILT: 48½" × 54½"

MATERIALS

Yardage is based on 42"-wide fabric.

⅞ yard of linen dot for blocks
¾ yard of cream solid for blocks
½ yard of ivory solid for blocks
⅓ yard of cream-and-black shirting for blocks
⅓ yard of light taupe print for blocks
⅓ yard of dark taupe print for blocks
⅛ yard of green print for blocks
⅛ yard of black script print for blocks
⅝ yard of black dot for blocks and binding
3⅛ yards of fabric for backing
55" × 61" piece of batting
24 black buttons in assorted sizes
Cosmo solid floss in charcoal #895
Eleganza pearl cotton #8 in Carbon #EZM04
Ellana wool thread in Charcoal #EN06
Black Pigma Micron pen .01 (fine tip)

CUTTING

From the linen dot, cut:
36 rectangles, 2½" × 8½"
12 rectangles, 2½" × 4½"

From the cream solid, cut:
36 rectangles, 2½" × 8½"

From the ivory solid, cut:
12 squares, 6½" × 6½"

From the black dot, cut:
12 squares, 2½" × 2½"
6 strips, 2½" × 42"

From the cream-and-black shirting, cut:
12 rectangles, 4½" × 6½"

From the light taupe print, cut:
6 rectangles, 4½" × 6½"
6 squares, 4½" × 4½"

From the dark taupe print, cut:
6 rectangles, 4½" × 6½"
6 squares, 4½" × 4½"

From the green print, cut:
12 squares, 2½" × 2½"

From the black script print, cut:
12 squares, 2½" × 2½"

FLOSS GUIDE

Use two strands of floss for all stitching unless otherwise noted. To use the wool thread, cut approximately 24" of floss, double the thread in the needle, and knot the two ends together. Using shorter thread helps prevent fraying.

✖ **Carbon pearl cotton:** Single olive branch veins (one strand), double olive branch stems (one strand)

✖ **Charcoal wool:** Single and double olive branches

✖ **Charcoal cotton floss:** Monograms, numbers, letters

MAKING THE BLOCKS

Use a ¼" seam allowance. Press the seam allowances as shown by the arrows in the illustrations.

1. Join a linen dot 2½" × 8½" rectangle to a cream solid 2½" × 8½" rectangle. Stitch a light taupe 4½" square to the right edge of the unit as shown to complete unit A, which should measure 4½" × 12½", including seam allowances. Make six of unit A with light taupe squares and six with dark taupe squares. (12 total).

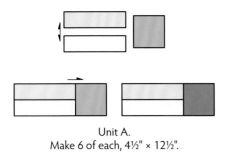

Unit A.
Make 6 of each, 4½" × 12½".

2. Join one shirting 4½" × 6½" rectangle, one linen dot 2½" × 4½" rectangle, and one dark taupe 4½" × 6½" rectangle into a vertical row to complete unit B. Unit B should measure 4½" × 14½", including seam allowances. Make six of unit B with dark taupe 4½" × 6½" rectangles and six with light taupe rectangles (12 total).

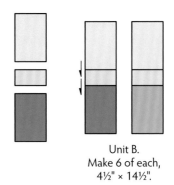

Unit B.
Make 6 of each,
4½" × 14½".

3. Join a linen dot 2½" × 8½" rectangle to a cream solid 2½" × 8½" rectangle to complete unit C. Unit C should measure 4½" × 8½", including seam allowances. Make 24 of unit C.

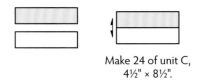

Make 24 of unit C,
4½" × 8½".

4. Join one black dot 2½" square, one green 2½" square, and one black script 2½" square in a vertical row. Stitch an ivory solid 6½" square to the right edge of the unit to complete unit D. Unit D should measure 6½" × 8½", including seam allowances. Make 12 of unit D.

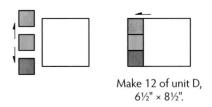

Make 12 of unit D,
6½" × 8½".

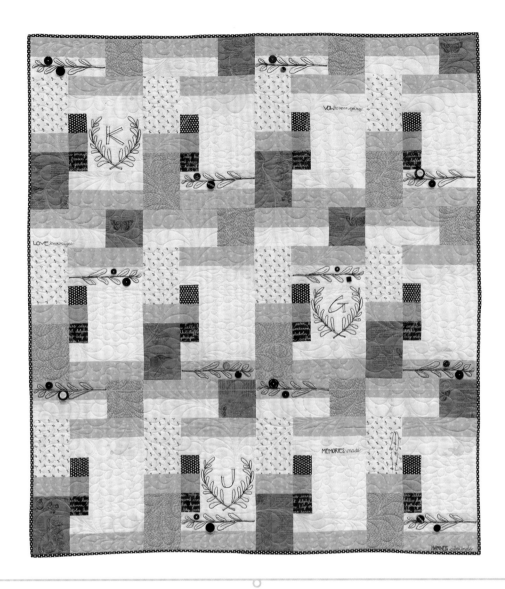

5. Join a C unit to the top and bottom of unit D as shown. Then stitch a dark unit B to the left side and a light unit A to the top to complete block A. Block A should measure 12½" × 18½", including seam allowances. Repeat to make six of block A.

6. Repeat step 5, switching the places of the light and dark taupe fabrics in units A and B, to make six of block B. Block B should measure 12½" × 18½", including seam allowances.

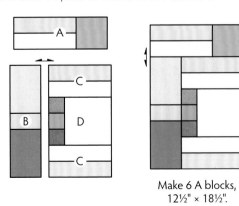

Make 6 A blocks,
12½" × 18½".

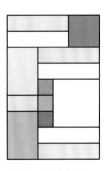

Make 6 B blocks,
12½" × 18½".

1. Using the Pigma pen, trace the embroidery details (with the aid of a light box) onto the finished blocks. Referring to the photo on page 53, hand embroider each block. For specific floss colors, refer to the "Floss Guide" on page 52. If desired, you can stitch more or fewer double olive branches to vary the number of included monograms, or add other special things that you'd like to represent in your quilt. If you're having friends and loved ones autograph the quilt, consider how much room you'll need to leave before adding the single olive branches.

2. Once the embroidery is complete, press all the blocks flat.

ASSEMBLING THE QUILT TOP

Lay out the quilt blocks into three rows of four blocks each. Join the blocks into rows, and then sew the rows together. The quilt top will measure 48½" × 54½".

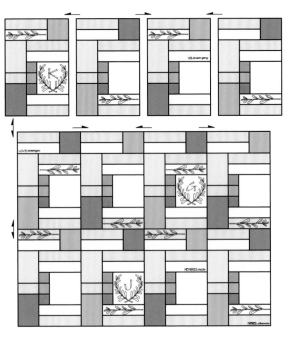

Quilt assembly

EMBROIDERING THE BLOCKS

The embroidery patterns are on pages 55 and 56. Refer to "Stitchery and Hand-Embroidery Basics" on page 72 for tracing tips. The embroidered letters and numbers are from the 2" alphabet on pages 77 and 78 and the quotes on page 55. Embroidery stitches are diagrammed on pages 73 and 74.

COURAGE BUILDER

I've found that with a little courage and my favorite pen, which is a black Pigma Micron pen .01, I can directly trace onto my freshly stitched block. This allows me to perfectly center the images onto the block. If you use a hoop when embroidering, you'll need a hot iron to press out all your wrinkles when you're done.

FINISHING THE QUILT

For more details on any finishing steps, visit ShopMartingale.com/HowtoQuilt for free, downloadable information.

1. Layer the quilt top, batting, and backing. Quilt by hand or machine. The quilt shown is machine quilted with dancing feathers and feather wreaths. Trim the excess batting and backing even with the quilt top.

2. Sew the black buttons to the single olive branches in each block. Refer to the photo on page 53 for placement.

3. Join the black dot 2½"-wide strips end to end to make one long strip. Use this strip to make double-fold binding and attach it to the quilt.

VINTAGE BUTTONS

I used vintage black buttons, sewn on after the quilt is complete, to represent the olives on the branch and give the quilt a nice textural feel. Make your quilt really special and use Grandma's black buttons from her button box.

VOW TO keep going

LOVE encourages

MEMORIES made

HAPPINESS abounds

Signed with Love Autograph Quilt

Embroidery Key
—— Backstitch

Signed with Love Autograph Quilt

Embroidery Key
——— Backstitch

GOOD HEART LOVE QUILT

Designed and made by Kori Turner-Goodhart. Quilted by Linda Sekerak

 The perfect couple in your life will forever cherish a quilt that celebrates their love. Hand embroidery beautifully complements the larger-scale blocks on this simple yet detailed quilt.

FINISHED QUILT: 60½" × 80½"

MATERIALS

Yardage is based on 42"-wide fabric. Fat quarters measure 18" × 21".

½ yard *each* of gray prints #1–#3 for rectangles*
⅝ yard of gray print #4 for rectangles
⅔ yard *each* of gray prints #5–#7 for rectangles
⅓ yard of gray print #8 for rectangles*
1 fat quarter *each* of gray prints #9 and #10 for rectangles
½ yard of coral stripe for appliqué hearts
⅜ yard of cream-and-gray dot for appliqué backgrounds
¼ yard *each* of cream dot and cream graph print for embroidery backgrounds
⅝ yard of red diagonal stripe for binding
4⅞ yards of fabric for backing
68" × 88" piece of batting
Cosmo Seasons variegated floss in mint green #5016; taupe #5028; green #5014; cardinal red #5005; coral #5004; and purple #8066

*If your gray prints #1 and #8 are less than 40½" wide after removing selvages, you'll need 1 yard of gray print #1 and ⅔ yard of gray print #8.

Cosmo solid floss in charcoal #895; graphite #893; gray #155; red #346; cranberry #858; orange #406; summer brown #716; moss green #2631; and plum #266
Black Pigma Micron pen .01 (fine tip)
Glue stick (optional)

CUTTING

From gray print #1, cut:
1 rectangle, 15½" × 40½" (J)

From gray print #2, cut:
1 rectangle, 15½" × 25½" (E)

From gray print #3, cut:
1 rectangle, 15½" × 30½" (F)

From gray print #4, cut:
3 rectangles, 5½" × 10½" (C)
3 rectangles, 5½" × 15½" (B)
1 rectangle, 5½" × 20½" (K)

From gray print #5, cut:
1 rectangle, 20½" × 25½" (G)

From gray print #6, cut:
1 rectangle, 20½" × 25½" (D)

From gray print #7, cut:
1 rectangle, 20½" × 30½" (A)

From gray print #8, cut:
1 rectangle, 10½" × 40½" (L)

Continued on page 59

Continued from page 57

From gray print #9, cut:
1 rectangle, 10½" × 20½" (H)

From gray print #10, cut:
1 rectangle, 10½" × 20½" (I)

From the cream-and-gray dot, cut:
10 squares, 5½" × 5½"

From the cream dot, cut:
5 squares, 7½" × 7½"

From the cream graph print, cut:
5 squares, 7½" × 7½"

From the red diagonal stripe, cut:
8 strips, 2½" × 42"

Floss Guide

Use two strands of floss for all stitching unless otherwise noted.

- Cardinal red: Bird wings, bird tail feathers (two wraps), heart in letter *o*, letter *L* dots (four wraps)
- Charcoal: All block frames, line through tic-tac-toe hearts, bird eyes (two wraps with one strand)
- Coral: Tic-tac-toe hearts
- Cranberry: Bird bellies
- Graphite: Tic-tac-toe *X*s
- Gray: Tic-tac-toe graph, *Love* lettering and accents
- Green: Grassy hill, flower leaves, flower leaf veins, flower swirls, flower stems
- Mint green: Clouds, heart cloud
- Moss green: Flower stem (three strands)
- Orange: Bird beaks (one strand)
- Plum: Tulip head accent, tulip dots (four wraps)
- Purple: Tulip head outline, tulip head top
- Red: Bird bodies
- Summer brown: Bird legs
- Taupe: Birds in sky

Making the Heart Blocks

The appliqué pattern is on page 63. Refer to "Stitch-and-Flip Appliqué" on page 75 for detailed information, or prepare the appliqué shapes for stitching using your favorite method.

1. Cut and prepare 10 heart appliqués from the coral stripe.

2. Fold each cream-and-gray 5½" square in half horizontally and vertically to create creases for placement. Lay out one heart appliqué on each square, referring to the appliqué placement guide. Pin or use a glue stick to secure the appliqué for stitching.

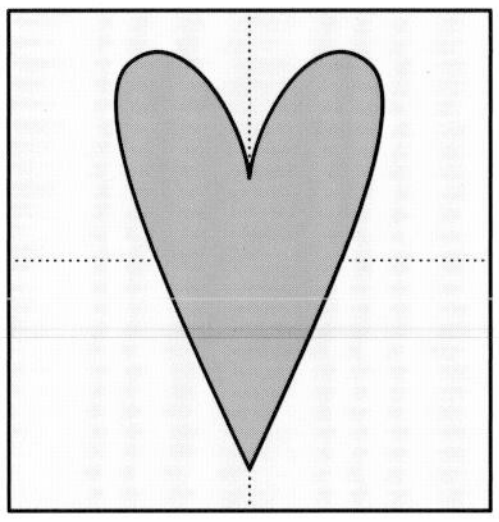

Appliqué placement

3. Hand appliqué the hearts to the backgrounds and press flat to complete 10 Heart blocks.

Making the Embroidered Blocks

The embroidery patterns are on pages 64 and 65. Embroidery stitches are diagrammed on pages 73 and 74.

1. Trace the embroidery patterns onto the 10 cream 7½" squares, referring to "Stitchery and Hand-Embroidery Basics" on page 72 for tracing tips. I used three birds, three tulips, two tic-tac-toes, and two *Love* squares. Following the embroidery guides on pages 64 and 65, hand embroider each block. For specific floss colors, refer to the "Floss Guide" at left.

2. Once all the embroidery is complete, press the squares flat; trim to 5½" square, keeping the designs centered, to complete 10 embroidered blocks.

ASSEMBLING THE QUILT Top

Use a ¼" seam allowance. Press the seam allowances as shown by the arrows in the illustrations.

1. Join one Heart block, one embroidered tic-tac-toe block, one embroidered bird block, and a B rectangle into a horizontal row. Stitch the row to the top of the A rectangle to complete unit 1, which should measure 25½" × 30½", including seam allowances.

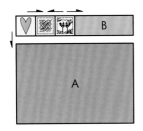

Unit 1,
25½" × 30½".

2. Join one Heart block, one embroidered tulip block, and a B rectangle into a horizontal row. Stitch the row to the bottom of the D rectangle. Join one Heart block, one embroidered tulip block, one embroidered *Love* block, and a C rectangle into a vertical row. Stitch this row to the left side of the unit to complete unit 2, which should measure 25½" × 30½", including seam allowances.

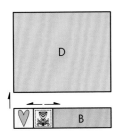

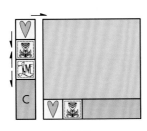

Unit 2,
25½" × 30½".

3. Join one embroidered bird block, one Heart block, one embroidered tic-tac-toe block, and a C rectangle into a vertical row. Stitch the row to the right edge of the E rectangle to complete unit 3, which should measure 20½" × 25½", including seam allowances.

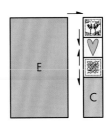

Unit 3,
20½" × 25½".

4. Join two Heart blocks, the remaining B rectangle, and one *Love* block into a vertical row. Stitch the row to the left side of the F rectangle to complete unit 4, which should measure 20½" × 30½", including seam allowances.

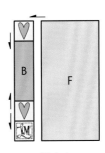

Unit 4,
20½" × 30½".

5. Join the remaining C rectangle, one Heart block, and one embroidered tulip block in a vertical row. Stitch the row between the H and I rectangles. Join the G rectangle to the top of the unit, then join the J rectangle to the right of the unit to complete unit 5, which should measure 40½" square, including seam allowances.

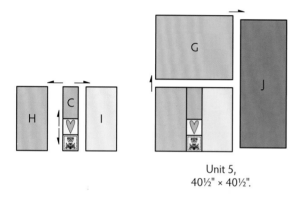

Unit 5,
40½" × 40½".

6. Join the K rectangle, three Heart blocks, and one embroidered bird block in a horizontal row. Stitch the L rectangle to the bottom to complete unit 6, which should measure 15½" × 40½", including seam allowances.

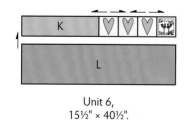

Unit 6,
15½" × 40½".

7. Referring to the quilt assembly diagram below, join units 1 and 2. Sew unit 3 to unit 4, and unit 5 to unit 6. Sew unit 3/4 to 5/6. Then join unit 1/2 to the top to complete the quilt top, which should measure 60½" × 80½", including seam allowances.

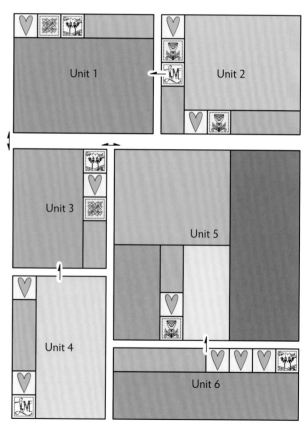

Quilt assembly

Stitched from the Heart

FINISHING THE QUILT

For more details on any finishing steps, visit ShopMartingale.com/HowtoQuilt for free, downloadable information.

1. Layer the quilt top, batting, and backing. Baste the layers together. Quilt by hand or machine. The quilt shown is machine quilted in traditional and organic feathers along with modern flowers. The embroidery and appliqué are outlined to enhance the designs. Trim the excess batting and backing even with the quilt top.

2. Join the red diagonal stripe 2½"-wide strips end to end to make one long strip to make double-fold binding and attach it to the quilt.

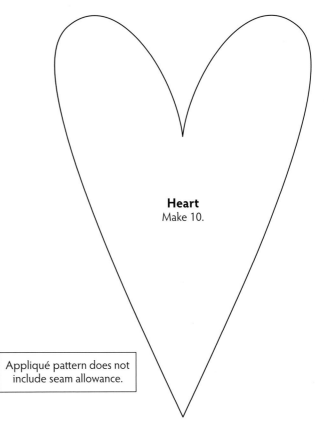

Heart
Make 10.

Appliqué pattern does not include seam allowance.

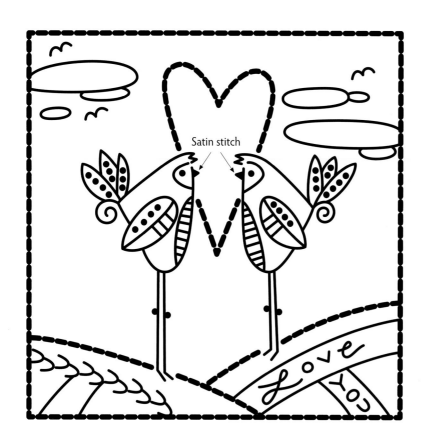

Good Heart Love Quilt

Embroidery Key

——————	Backstitch
▬ ▬ ▬	Chain stitch
﹥﹥﹥﹥	Feather stitch
●	French knot (4 wraps)
■	Satin stitch

Satin stitch

Embroidery Key

——————	Backstitch
▬ ▬ ▬	Chain stitch
●	French knot (4 wraps)

Stitched from the Heart

Good Heart Love Quilt

Embroidery Key

——	Backstitch
-----	Chain stitch
>>>>>	Feather stitch
- - -	Running stitch

Embroidery Key

——	Backstitch
-----	Chain stitch
>>>>>>	Fly stitch
●	French knot (4 wraps)

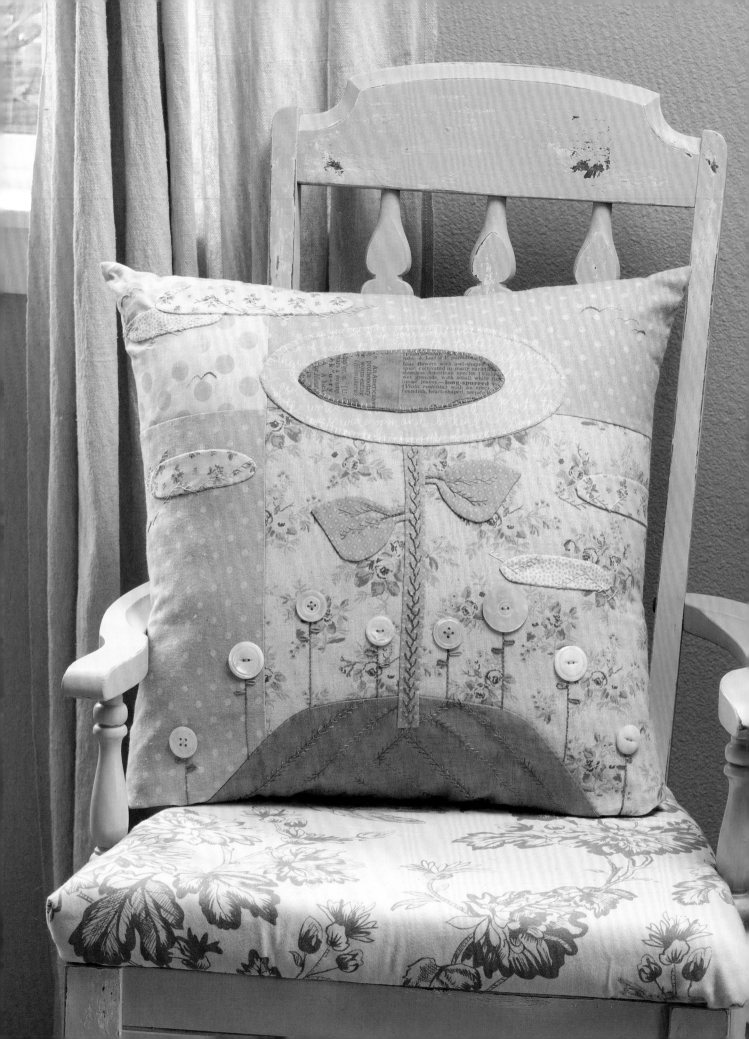

Be Yourself Pillow

Designed and made by Kori Turner-Goodhart.

Elevate a super simple patchwork pillow into special gift territory by adding a cheery sunflower reaching for the sky among a field of button buds, embroidered birds, and appliquéd clouds.

FINISHED PILLOW: 20" × 20"

Materials

Yardage is based on 42"-wide fabric.

½ yard of floral linen for pillow front and back
¼ yard of tan polka-dot linen for pillow front
½ yard of cream polka-dot linen for pillow front and back
11" × 11" square of yellow print for sunflower
8" × 8" square of brown print for sunflower center
12" × 14" rectangle of olive print for grassy hill
8" × 15" rectangle of blue floral for clouds
5" × 8" rectangle of blue dot for clouds
6" × 9" rectangle of light green dot for sunflower stem and leaves
1⅛ yards of muslin for pillow lining
20" × 20" pillow form
8 white buttons in assorted sizes for pillow front
Cosmo Seasons variegated floss in pink #8008; butter yellow #8027; mint green #5016; taupe #5028; and green #5014
Dazzle thread in Golden Oliver #4120
Black Pigma Micron pen .01 (fine tip)
Glue stick (optional)

Cutting

From the floral linen, cut:
1 square, 14½" × 14½"
1 rectangle, 16" × 20½"

From the tan polka-dot linen, cut:
2 rectangles, 6½" × 14½"

From the cream polka-dot linen, cut:
1 rectangle, 16" × 20½"
1 square, 6½" × 6½"

From the light green dot, cut:
1 strip, 1¼" × 9"

From the muslin, cut:
1 square, 20½" × 20½"
2 rectangles, 16" × 20½"

Floss Guide

Use two strands of floss for all stitching unless otherwise noted.

- Butter yellow: Sunflower outline
- Golden Oliver: Sunflower stem details (one strand), grassy hill details, button flower stems and leaves
- Green: Leaf details, grassy hill details, words embroidered on hill, button flower stems
- Mint green: Cloud accents
- Pink: Securing buttons
- Taupe: Sunflower center outline, birds

PIECING THE PILLOW FRONT

Use a ¼" seam allowance. Press the seam allowances as shown by the arrows in the illustrations.

Lay out the cream polka-dot square, the two tan polka-dot rectangles, and the floral square in two rows of two. Sew the pieces together in each row. Join the rows to make the pillow front that measures 20½" square, including seam allowances.

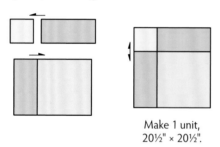

Make 1 unit,
20½" × 20½".

APPLIQUÉING AND EMBROIDERING THE PILLOW FRONT

The appliqué patterns are on pages 70 and 71. Refer to "Stitch-and-Flip Appliqué" on page 75 for detailed information, or prepare your appliqué shapes for stitching using your favorite method. Refer to "Stitchery and Hand-Embroidery Basics" on page 72 for tracing tips. For specific floss colors, refer to the "Floss Guide" on page 67. Embroidery stitches are diagrammed on pages 73 and 74.

1. Cut and prepare the sunflower, leaf, and cloud appliqués as noted on the patterns.

2. Trace the hill appliqué to the right side of the olive rectangle. Before cutting out, trace the saying *be you* to finish ¼" left of center and ½" from the bottom of the hill, and then trace the grass lines. Create the hill appliqué and embroider.

3. Use the light green dot 1¼" × 9" strip to make a ⅝" × 7⅝" stem as shown.

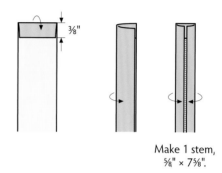

⅜"

Make 1 stem,
⅝" × 7⅝".

4. Place the prepared appliqués on the pieced pillow front. Note that cloud B extends off the right edge; trim the excess once attached. Place the finished end of the sunflower stem on top of the grassy hill as shown, overlapping the hill by 1". Tuck the top raw end of the stem approximately ⅜" under the bottom of the sunflower appliqué; trim the top of the stem if necessary. Tuck the leaf ends under the stem sides. Pin or use a glue stick to secure all of the appliqués for stitching.

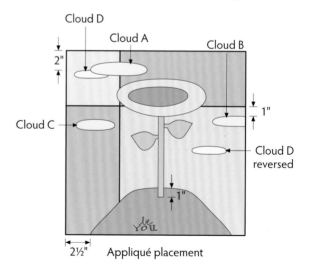

Appliqué placement

5. Hand appliqué all the pieces to the pillow front and press flat. Mark and stitch the remaining embroidery details on the pillow front. Use a fly stitch for the grass lines on the hill. Once the embroidery is complete, press the pillow front flat.

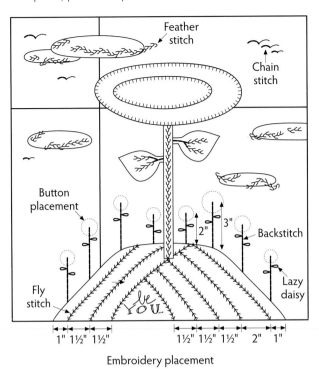

Embroidery placement

6. Layer the finished pillow front, wrong sides together, on the 20½" muslin square and stitch around the layers, ⅛" inside the perimeter. The muslin inner layer will protect the back of your embroidery stitches.

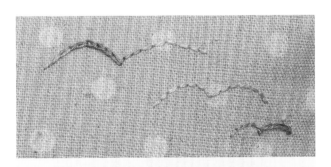

HOW MANY BIRDS IN YOUR FLOCK?

I have six members in my family, so that's how many birds I stitched in my sky! One wing of each bird is chain stitched, and the other is backstitched. If you're making a pillow for a friend, trace as many birds as you need for her flock.

MAKING THE PILLOW BACK

Following are instructions for a simple envelope-style pillow back. For instructions to make a buttoned pillow back that includes an embroidered message, visit ShopMartingale.com/StitchedfromtheHeart.

1. Layer floral and muslin 16" × 20½" rectangles, wrong sides together, and stitch around the perimeter with a ⅛" seam allowance. Repeat for the cream polka-dot linen and second muslin 16" × 20½" rectangles.

2. Along one long edge of each layered 16" × 20½" rectangle, fold under the edge ½", press, and then fold over another 1"; press again. Stitch along the folded edge for a neat finish.

3. Place the completed pillow front on a flat surface, right side up. Place the floral backing piece right side down on the pillow front, matching the raw edges at the top and sides. The hemmed edge should run along the front horizontally. Layer the polka-dot backing right side down so the finished edge overlaps the floral backing and the raw edges align with the pillow-front edges. Pin through all layers and stitch around the pillow with a ¼" seam allowance. Snip off the seam allowances at all four corners as shown.

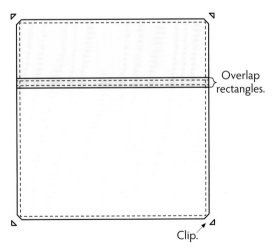

Overlap rectangles.

Clip.

4. Turn the pillow cover right side out through the opening. Carefully push out the corners. Press, then sew a button at the top of each embroidered stem.

5. Insert a 20"-square pillow form.

Sunflower
Make 1 from yellow print.

Sunflower center
Make 1 from brown print.

Sunflower leaf
Make 1 and 1 reversed
from light green dot.

be YOU...

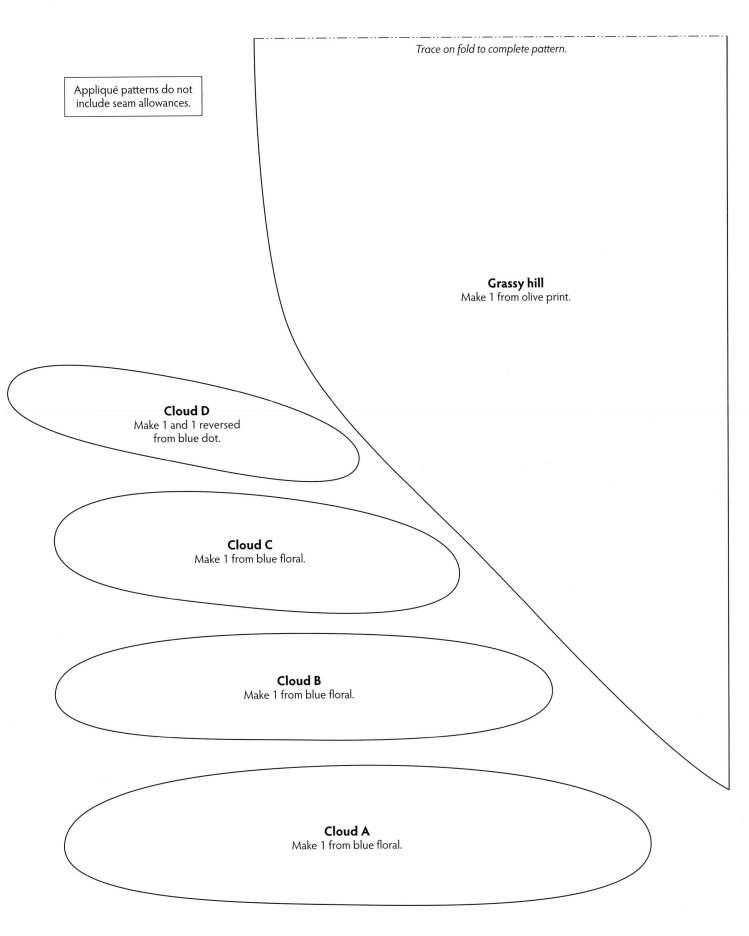

Appliqué patterns do not include seam allowances.

Trace on fold to complete pattern.

Grassy hill
Make 1 from olive print.

Cloud D
Make 1 and 1 reversed
from blue dot.

Cloud C
Make 1 from blue floral.

Cloud B
Make 1 from blue floral.

Cloud A
Make 1 from blue floral.

Be Yourself Pillow

Stitchery and Hand-Embroidery Basics

The information in this section is designed to make the embroidery process fun and painless.

Tracing and Stitching Tips

✖ Make sure your fabric is pressed flat before transferring the pattern.

✖ For these projects, I traced my embroidery designs using a light box, which allowed me to see through several layers. I use a .01 (fine tip) black Pigma Micron pen for tracing. This is permanent—if you're not comfortable with that, use a removable marking pen with a fine tip.

✖ If you're without a light box, a window should suffice for single-layer tracing. For appliqués, tape the traced pattern to a window. Position the corresponding fabric right side down against the pattern and trace the outline of the appliqué motif onto the wrong side of the fabric. Do not cut out. Flip the traced appliqué piece over and trace any corresponding embroidery onto the right side of each piece. Complete your appliqués using the "Stitch-and-Flip Appliqué" technique (page 75). Trace any embroidery onto your background, stitch the appliqués in place, and embroider.

✖ For basic embroidery, I use a hoop. I find that a 3½" to 5" size works best. A small hoop allows your hands to have more control and lets you focus on specific areas of stitching. I don't use a hoop for adding embellishments. If you're embroidering on a finished block, be particularly careful not to stretch or break any stitches when putting the block in the hoop. A hot iron should take care of any wrinkles after embroidering.

✖ I use a #7 or #8 embroidery needle for six-strand floss. For heavier threads like pearl cotton and Dazzle thread, I use a #24 chenille needle.

BASIC SUPPLIES FOR EMBROIDERY

A wonderful thing about embroidery is it doesn't require a lot of special tools. I used these basic supplies for the projects in this book.

- *Black Pigma Micron pen .01*
- *Fabric glue stick*
- *Appliqué pins*
- *#7 or #8 embroidery needles*
- *#24 chenille needles*
- *Light box*

EMBROIDERY STITCHES

The stitches I used throughout the book are relatively common and easy to master. However, there are countless embroidery stitches you may prefer to use, especially when embellishing the Crazy hearts on the "Heart of the Family Banner" on page 43. Visit ShopMartingale.com/HowtoQuilt to see more stitches.

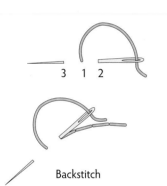

Backstitch

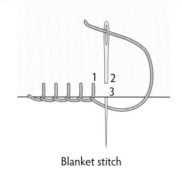

Blanket stitch

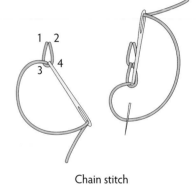

Chain stitch

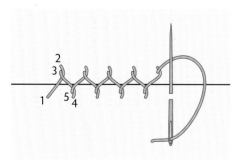

Cretan stitch

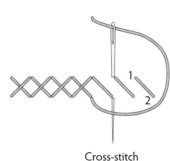

Cross-stitch

Feather stitch

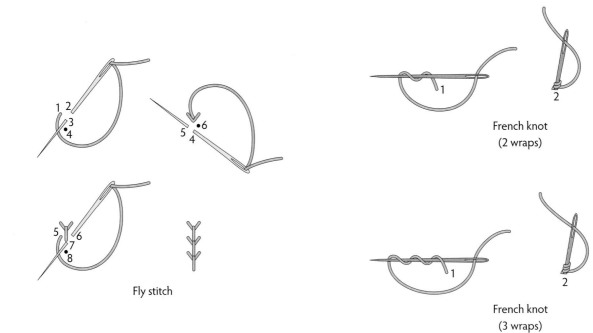

French knot
(2 wraps)

Fly stitch

French knot
(3 wraps)

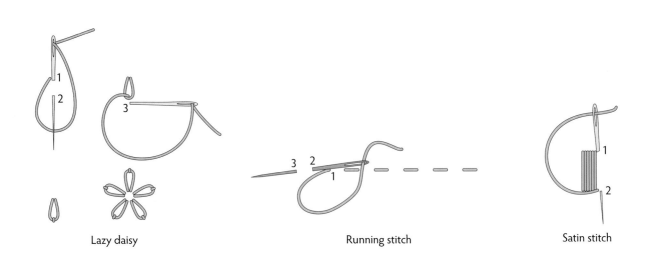

Lazy daisy

Running stitch

Satin stitch

Stitch-and-Flip Appliqué

The perfectionist in me wants my appliqué shapes to be exactly like the pattern. My mom taught me a method that I love. We call it the Stitch-and-Flip method. This technique uses a little extra fabric and takes a little extra time, but your appliqué shapes will come out impeccably. The reason for the extra fabric is to hide any show-through (where you can see the background fabric through the appliqué shape), and also to mimic the look of needle-turn appliqué. Try it—I think you'll love how it looks.

1. Make templates for the appliqué patterns. I prefer cardstock, but you could also use template plastic. First, trace the patterns onto plain white copy paper using a fine-tip permanent pen. Second, use a glue stick to glue the copy paper to the cardstock. Then cut out the shapes on the drawn line.

2. You'll need a piece of fabric that's big enough to fold in half and still accommodate your appliqué shape. For our example, a circle with a 2" diameter, we'll need an approximate 3" × 6" rectangle of fabric.

3. Fold the rectangle of fabric in half, right sides together.

4. Center and trace the shape onto the folded fabric with a .01 Pigma pen.

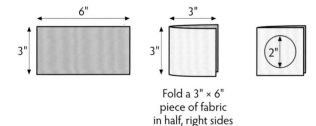

Fold a 3" × 6" piece of fabric in half, right sides together.

5. Sew directly on the line with your sewing machine.

Machine stitch directly on traced line.

6. Cut out the shape, ⅛" beyond the sewing line. Carefully make a slit through the center of *one* of the fabric layers.

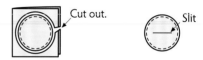

Cut out.   Slit

7. With small, sharp scissors, take little snips into the seam allowance around the perimeter of the shape. Turn the shape inside out through the slit.

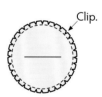

Clip.

8. To make crisp edges, use small, sharp scissors on the inside of the shape to gently press into the seams. Take your time, being very careful to not rip a hole in the seam. Iron the shape on the back, then the front.

Glide back and forth on inside of seam gently for crisp edge.

Alphabet Patterns

To customize your projects, I've provided patterns for letters ranging in size from ¾" to 2". Follow these steps to make an embroidery pattern using the letters.

1. On a plain sheet of white copy paper, draw two perpendicular lines that represent the height of your letters that you'll be tracing onto fabric.

2. Trace the letters that spell out your words between the drawn lines with a thick black marker. If the text is too long for one sheet of paper, join two sheets with tape and extend the perpendicular lines.

Draw 2 parallel lines on paper, spaced the desired height of letters.

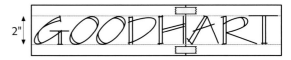

If words are too long, tape 2 pieces of paper together. Again, draw 2 lines.

3. Place the letters on a light box and trace your words onto the fabric.

9. Using a fabric glue stick, glide a little glue onto the back of the appliqué shape and place it in the desired area. Use appliqué pins to pin the shape to the background for extra stability.

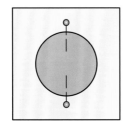

Glide glue on back of shape.

Glue shape in place and pin.

10. Using a traditional appliqué stitch (blind stitch), stitch the shape in place. For more information about this stitch and other appliqué techniques, visit ShopMartingale.com/HowtoQuilt.

Stitchery and Hand-Embroidery Basics

Stitched from the Heart

½" Alphabet

A B C D E F G H I
J K L M N O P Q R
S T U V W X Y Z

2" Numbers

1 2 3 4 5 6 7 8 9 0

½" Numbers

1 2 3 4 5 6 7 8 9 0

RESOURCES

Lecien Cosmo Flosses
OliveGraceStudios.com

Eleganza Pearl Cotton,
Ellana Wool Thread, and Dazzle Threads
SueSpargo.com

ACKNOWLEDGMENTS

Thanks to the following for helping with the projects:

- ✖ Cathy Turner, my mom, for helping bring each of these projects to life.

- ✖ Janet Grace Everett, my great-grandmother, for sewing on bindings and being the namesake of my little business.

- ✖ Linda Sekerak of Cottage Garden Quilts, Medina, Ohio, and Rebecca Silbaugh of Ruby Blue Quilting Studio, Painesville, Ohio. Thank you both for your beautiful machine quilting, expertise, and for fitting me into your busy schedules.

About the Author

Kori is a dreamer, designer, and quilt-shop owner. She received a BFA in interior design from the Savannah College of Art and Design in Savannah, Georgia. In the corporate world she designed everything from retail interiors to education facilities while living and working in Columbus, Ohio, and Washington, D.C. After moving around, she came back to her farm-girl roots in northeast Ohio. In 2009 she opened a quilt shop, Olive Grace Studios, and started designing patterns.

Through her patterns, Kori strives to honor the people she has loved and lost and the places she has been, which is what makes her designs and business practices unique. Because she's always thinking about the cherished people in her life, her quilts and other fun designs are made out of love!

Kori says, "I'm a heart girl, and I hope that when people get to know me and see my work, they get that feeling."

Visit Kori at OliveGraceStudios.com.